FAMILY STRUCTURE
BY CHOICE

A Defense of Traditional Marriage Structure

Daniel Ukadike Nwaelene, ThD

FAMILY STRUCTURE BY CHOICE: A DEFENSE OF TRADITIONAL MARRIAGE STRUCTURE

Daniel Nwaelene Books, LLC
190 Palisade Ave #4D
Yonkers, NY 10703, USA
www.danielnwaelenebooksllc.com
914 282-0120

ISBN: 979-8-9922386-5-5 (sc)
ISBN: 979-8-9922386-6-2 (hb)
ISBN: 979-8-9922386-7-9 (e)

BOOKS BY THE AUTHOR

1. JESUS CHRIST: Savior, Judge and King of the World

Originally published by: WestBow Press Year: 2017.
www.westbowpress.com Tel.: +1 866 928 1240.
Re-published by: Bookside Press www.booksidepress.com – Year:
2024.
Tel. 1 877 741 8091.

2. ACTING MOVIE SCRIPTS OR FULFILLING PROPHECIES?

Originally Published by: Christian Faith Publishing, Inc. – Year: 2018.
www.christianfaithpublishing.com
Re-published by: Daniel Nwaelene Books – Year: 2024
https://danielnwaelenebooksllc.com/ Tel: +1 914 920 9862.

3. FAMILY STRUCTURE BY CHOICE: A Defense of Traditional
    Marriage Structure

Originally published by: iUniverse Publishing - Year: 2020
www.iuniverse.com Tel.: +1 800 288 4677
Re-published by: Gotham Books, Inc
https://gothambooksinc.com Year: 2022 Tel: +1 307 404 7800.

4. GOD IS INTERESTED IN YOUR MARRIAGE: Path to a
    Successful, Happy Christian

Marriage
Originally published by: Gotham Books, Inc. - Year: 2024
https://gothambooksinc.com Tel: +1 307 404 7800.

5. MONEY, POWER AND SEX: The Implication of Money, Power
and Sex In The Downfall of People
Published by Daniel Nwaelene Books, LLC. – Year: 2025
https://danielnwaelenebooksllc.com/ Tel: +1 914 920 9862.

Authorized (King James) Version (AKJV)

CONTENTS

Abbreviations of Bible Versions Quoted

KJV	King James Version
BSB	Berean Study Bible
CEV	Contemporary English Version
CSB	Christian Standard Bible
DRAB	Douay–Rheims, 1899 US edition
ESV	English Standard Version
GNT	Good News Translation
GWT	God's Word Translation
HCSB	Holman Christian Standard Bible
ISV	International Standard Version
NETB	New English Translation
NIV	New International Version
NKJV	New King James Version
NLT	New Living Translation
NLV	New Life Version
WNT	Weymouth New Testament
YLT	Young's Literal Translation

To my family:

My dear wife, Patricia Ifeanyi Nwaelene (née Ojei) and
our children (also sons and daughters of God in Christ Jesus), who,
while growing up, gave us no causes
for anxiety, to the glory of God:
Chiedu
Umeadim
Ebelechukwu
Ijeoma

This book is also a tribute to my father, Rev. Sylvanus Nwani
Nwaelene. He and his late wife (my mother) were married and lived
together for twenty-four years before his wife's death "did them
part." In spite of the fear of his future loneliness entertained by the
children, my father was determined not to remarry so that he would
not be distracted from giving all his children the care and training he
and his late wife had planned and desired to give us. He said that
another woman would not take care of his children well and was
likely to bring a division between him and his children. He could not
be persuaded otherwise. He is now ninety-seven years old and does
not regret his decision. He remained faithful to his vow and to his wife
and remained a blessing to all his children. To God be the glory on
his behalf.

FOREWORD

I CONSIDER IT A GREAT HONOR TO HAVE BEEN ASKED to write the foreword to this book written by my friend and brother Rev. Dr. Dan Ukadike Nwaelene. My earliest contact with Dan was way back when we were growing up in Issele-Uku, in the Delta State of Nigeria. We were both members of the Pilgrim Baptist Church, Issele-Uku. His parents were staunch members of the church. We both went our separate ways only to come together much later as members of the New Estate Baptist Church in Suru-Lere, Lagos. We were both members of the men's fellowship of that church. Dan showed signs of being a committed follower of the Lord and Savior Jesus Christ. My duty here is to tell you why you should go get a copy of this book and read it for yourself. If my testimony is correct, you then have the duty to recommend it to others!

In this his latest book, Dan has done what Christian writers are admonished to do—explain what the Holy Bible says concerning the subject they have chosen to write about. Many other writers expound on their personal opinion and comb the Bible to find some passages, including those with little or no relevance, to support their opinions. Some propagate psychology theories and find Bible passages to support their positions. Not so with Dan, particularly in this book!

Though the author chose a title that screams family, the bulk of the work is on marriage because marriage is the highway to the family. He clearly states in his preface: "This book is, therefore, meant to point the reader in the right direction in order to prevent errors in choosing the kind of structure to have, or where to make possible corrections—depending on your current status."

Dan's argument is that God, who created mankind and the universe, had a plan and purpose for His creation. In His infinite wisdom He made mankind in His image and likeness and gave them dominion over the rest of creation. To accomplish this role, mankind had to be organized into societies and multiply. Therefore, God ordained marriage to ensure the continuity and orderliness of society. Marriage as ordained by God has a clearly defined structure and guidelines. The author uses several Bible passages to show that Satan, as the enemy of God, has continued to wage war on the family in order to derail the plan of God for society. This is Satan's mission, which started when he deceived Adam and Eve in the Garden of Eden.

The author discusses the various family structures that mankind has created since the fall. These include polygamy, polyandry, and gay family or same-sex marriage. Others include single-parent family, cohabitation, and some types that cannot easily fall into any of the aforementioned categories.

Dan goes into some detail to explain some of the reasons often given for each of these anomalous situations. In his view, while such reasons explain the choice of such structures, they are at best mere excuses and not a solid defense of defiant behaviors! No such defense is acceptable to God for contravening His laid-down commandments for His creation.

The author discusses from the biblical perspective the issue of remaining unmarried and concludes that such a choice must be based on spiritual consideration.

The author applies the teachings of the Bible, from the Old Testament to the New Testament, to instruct on how to handle many of the challenges couples face. His advice is that couples need the Holy Spirit to make a success of their marriage.

I believe strongly that this book was inspired by the Holy Spirit at a time such as this, when there is a war on the family. The enemy knows that the family is the foundation of society, and as the family goes, so goes the society. This is the reason for the onslaught against the family. Therefore, you need to read this book to understand the schemes of the enemy against you. Then you will be able to put on the whole armor of God to fight the battle. That is how your marriage and family can flourish!

Rev. Dr. Ben Nnaemeka Nwaochei
Executive Pastor
Adelphi Bible Baptist Church
Adelphi, Maryland, USA

PREFACE

ISSUES CONCERNING CHOICE OF FAMILY STRUCTURES are both social and spiritual. The kinds of choices that people make these days cause onlookers with *educated* minds to get worried. They bring to mind the observation of the Lord that His people perished for lack of knowledge. He said, "My people are destroyed for lack of knowledge: because thou hast rejected knowledge, I will also reject thee, that thou shalt be no priest to me: seeing thou hast forgotten the law of thy God, I will also forget thy children" (Hosea 4:6). Some people do things because others do, without counting cost. Every choice one makes has eternal consequences: whom to worship and serve, either the almighty God or the devil (no sitting on the fence); whether or not to marry; whom to get married to; whether or not to bear children; how to live your life; and many more choices.

Family Structure by Choice is not just about making choices; it is also aimed at presenting the kinds of family structures that are prevalent in the world today in comparison to the original family structure as God designed and ordained it. To be able to detect a counterfeit, one must know the original very well. In effect, many people may not know wrong family structures because they do not know God's choice of family structure.

Family Structure by Choice is, therefore, meant to point the reader in the right direction in order to prevent errors in choosing the kind of structure to have, or in order to make possible corrections depending on one's current marital status. However, "with God nothing shall be impossible" (Luke 1:37). Jesus also said, "The things which are impossible with men are possible with God" (Luke 18:27).

The views expressed here are based on the Holy Bible, "the word of God [which] is quick, and powerful, and sharper than any twoedged sword, piercing even to the dividing asunder of soul and spirit, and of the joints and marrow, and is a discerner of the thoughts and intents of the heart" (Hebrews 4:12).

Every serious manufacturer of things meant for general use or consumption provides a user's manual. Since God is the Author of marriage, His user's manual for marriage is found in His Word. Note that in view of this author's observation, most Bible references in books are usually skipped and never read. Bible references in *Family Structure by Choice* are fully quoted to give opportunities to the reader to read the direct words of the Bible.

You are hereby encouraged not to jump to conclusions but to patiently read through the book with an open mind. If you do so, you shall be blessed. You will never regret any time you invest in this pursuit.

ACKNOWLEDGMENTS

I OWE A GREAT DEAL OF GRATITUDE TO MANY FOR THE production of this book. First, I give thanks to the almighty God for enabling me to start and finish the work. No matter how brief a book may be, without the inspiration and guidance of God, writing it is a failure ab initio. The Bible says in Psalm 127:1, "Except the Lord build the house, they labor in vain that build it. Except the Lord keep the city, the watchman waketh but in vain." The success of any good project depends on the blessing of God. God is ever faithful.

My gratitude also goes in no small measure to the authors and publishers of books and other documents referenced in this work for allowing their works to be quoted or referenced. Though all or, at least, most of these references have been duly acknowledged as footnotes and in the bibliography, they deserve some special appreciation at this point.

I thank my friend, big Christian brother, and erstwhile work colleague Mr. Roland Bishop Jr. for his encouragement at the initial stages of putting this work together. I also appreciate my wife, Patricia, for her usual cooperation and ideas reflected in this write-up, as well as every other person who contributed in one way or another to making the publishing of this book a reality. This includes the publisher of this book, iUniverse, and Rev. Dr. Ben Nnaemeka Nwaochei for taking time out of his busy schedule to read through the draft of this work and agreeing to write the foreword for it. Thank you, sir.

Reader, thank you for making time to read this book. I believe and pray that your sacrifice shall be worthwhile in the end and a blessing to you and your generation, notwithstanding that the work is an imperfect one written by an imperfect man. The Bible says, "God purposely chose what the world considers nonsense in order to shame the wise, and he chose what the world considers weak in order to shame the powerful" (1 Corinthians 1:27 GNT). Thank you once again for reading through and recommending this book to someone else you care about.

Rev. Daniel Ukadike Nwaelene, ThD
Yonkers, New York
April 2019

CHAPTER 1

INTRODUCTION

ON THE STREETS OF NEW YORK IN PARTICULAR, AND IN
the USA in general, you find billboards advertising services of
attorneys (lawyers) who can procure divorce for as low as $349. It has
become so cheap and easy to destroy a marriage, the institution that
costs so much time, money, and emotional and psychological
feelings. Marriage can be demolished for an infinitesimal amount of
legal fees. This is in spite of the fact that the Word of God says that
"they are thus no longer two but one flesh and as such *let not man
separate* what God has joined together" (Matthew 19:6; emphasis
added).

Some people have often said that the law was given exclusively to
Israel, and for that reason it is not applicable to, or binding on, the
gentiles who became Christians. It is true that the law was given to
Israel, yet it is known that God chose Israel to be a model nation to
the world. God said, "Seeing that Abraham shall surely become a
great and mighty nation, and all the nations of the earth shall be

blessed in him? For I know him, that he will command his children and his household after him, and they shall keep the way of the Lord, to do justice and judgment" (Genesis 18:18–19).

Along the same vein, people suggest that the Old Testament scriptures are not applicable to Christians. The purpose of these claims is to enable the claimants to sin and absolve themselves of sin. But they forget that Jesus Christ, "the Author and Perfecter of [the Christian] faith" (Hebrews 12:2 NASB), said that He came not to abolish the law but to fulfill it. He said the following:

Think not that I am come to destroy the law, or the prophets: I am not come to destroy, but to fulfil. For verily I say unto you, Till heaven and earth pass, one jot or one tittle shall in no wise pass from the law, till all be fulfilled. Whosoever therefore shall break one of these least commandments, and shall teach men so, he shall be called the least in the kingdom of heaven: but whosoever shall do and teach them, the same shall be called great in the kingdom of heaven. For I say unto you, That except your righteousness shall exceed the righteousness of the scribes and Pharisees, ye shall in no case enter into the kingdom of heaven. (Matthew 5:17–20)

Satan has from the days of Adam and Eve been working against God; turning God's creation, mankind, against God; and increasing his (the devil's) company in hellfire, his final destiny. When Saul (later Paul) was on his way to Damascus to round up people of the Way (Christians) and take them to Jerusalem, he encountered the Lord Jesus Christ. Jesus Christ asked Saul why he was persecuting Him. He told Saul that it is hard for him to kick against the pricks (Acts 9:5). Though this statement has been omitted in some Bible translations, it is very true that an attempt to kick against the pricks or the Solid Rock will only render one's legs destroyed. So it is with working against God's established structures, including the family.

The Bible

I believe and teach that the Bible is the inspired, inerrant, and infallible Word of God, which never expires; all the conclusions in this work are based on it. If the Bible is so (and of course it is), and because God does not and cannot lie, then His Word is trustworthy. The Bible says of itself, "All scripture is given by inspiration of God, and is profitable for doctrine, for reproof, for correction, for instruction in righteousness: That the man of God may be perfect, thoroughly furnished unto all good works" (2 Timothy 3:16–17).

Some of the many other passages in the Bible that discuss the Bible itself are as follows:

> *Jesus said that heaven and earth shall pass away, but His words shall not pass away unfulfilled (Matthew 24:35). He also said that people who hear the Word of God and keep it are rather blessed (Luke 11:28).*

The apostle John wrote that the world and the lust thereof pass away, but anyone that does the will of God abides forever (1 John 2:17).

> *For the word of God is quick, and powerful, and sharper than any twoedged sword, piercing even to the dividing asunder of soul and spirit, and of the joints and marrow, and is a discerner of the thoughts and intents of the heart. Neither is there any creature that is not manifest in his sight: but all things are naked and opened unto the eyes of him with whom we have to do. (Hebrews 4:12–13)*

Family

Until recently, anytime the word *family* was mentioned, the picture that immediately came to mind was of a group of persons comprising a father, a mother, a child or children, and in some cases, a servant or servants. The few occasions where the picture was different was when the family had lost by death one of the parents—father or mother. Of course, in some African and Middle Eastern countries there are families with more than one mother present, and children from such families are looked at with some degree of ignominy.

But these days it has become very common to have a family consisting of one non-widowed parent and his or her children. Many people now pride themselves, from their testimonies, in having been brought up by their single mothers. You don't often hear such testimonies if the single parent was the father. Some people sing the praises of their single parent notwithstanding how the parent's singleness was arrived at. A close look into the situation reveals that it is a reflection of so-called modern society.

Another common sight these days is step-relationships—stepfather, stepmother, stepson, stepdaughter, perhaps step-friends, and so forth. These arise from the remarriage of widowed and divorced parents. Things are changing rapidly! But God does not change, nor do His standards.

Unusual Happenings

While I was growing up in my village, it was uncommon for men to break into people's homes to steal. Stealing used to be of goats and sheep, of farm products, or trapped animals. Only one man, nicknamed Congo, was known to have broken into a few homes when men had gone to farm and women to market on market days. When he was discovered, he was banished from the town. Then, a group of five men went to other people's farms to steal. On a certain day, the town's monarch ordered the men to be openly flogged. That actually happened before I was born, but the story continued to be told.

By the time I went to high school—an all-boys' institution—I began to realize that there were other forms of evil practiced by

4

people, especially lying, cheating, and slandering. In a certain year, precisely 1965, there were instances of homosexual acts by one senior student with some freshman boys who were afraid to report him for fear of unnecessary punishment. The cases were handled secretly by the student administration without allowing them to reach the school authorities because, with the school being a Christian institution, it would have resulted in the expulsion of the senior student even though he was getting ready for his graduation examinations. It would have been a disaster for him. In the preceding year, a semi-senior student was expelled for putting the maid of the vice principal in the family way.

Smoking was prohibited in the school, but some students usually did it secretly at night in the surrounding bushes. However, anyone caught was disciplined. One student constantly exhibited acts of disobedience, indiscipline, and evil, for which the principal wrote on his testimonial that God had endowed him with wonderful intelligence, but the devil had denied him character. These things were happening among young men in their teens and early twenties to mid-twenties.

As time went on, there were additions to our vocabulary of such terms as *corruption, nepotism, tribalism, fraud*, and *favoritism*. These were issues that constituted the talk of town all over the nation, to the extent that there were military coups and countercoups that brought into power one new set of military personnel after the other. Each new set of coup plotters accused the government it had overthrown of all the aforementioned ills and more, yet they turned out to be no different from the people they overthrew. Up till the time of my writing this book, my country of origin, which is naturally endowed with mineral wealth, is very poor. In fact, a few individuals are said to be richer than the entire nation, while all others are wallowing in abject poverty. Greed and corruption are ravaging the nation. Youth unemployment is at its peak.

After the civil war in Nigeria (a.k.a. the Nigeria–Biafra War) that lasted some thirty months, we began to hear of such violent crimes as armed robbery resulting in murders, hired killings (also hired assassins), and kidnapping with the intent to collect ransom. Later, new sets of words and phrases were added to our vocabulary, including *drug pushing, drug peddling, currency and product counterfeiting,* and *money laundering.* All these and more were indicative of the presence of sin in the lives of the natural local people, manifesting in different forms—all signs of degeneration in the society's level of fear of God and knowledge of God. Though there were many upright people in the society, the terrible people in modern times make it look like everyone is evil.

I had thought that the situation described above, which is representative of what you find in all developing countries, especially in Africa, would be unheard of in the advanced or developed nations (the Western world). But not so! What you see and hear on television and read in newspapers on a daily basis in and about the Western nations includes pictures and stories of such evil acts as those listed in the foregoing paragraphs, but perpetrated in more sophisticated ways. You hear of murder, mass killings, rape, robbery, lying, racism (rather than tribalism), nepotism, disobedience to parents and constituted authority, total disrespect with impunity for elders, total disregard for God and godliness, oppression of the poor and helpless, homosexuality and lesbianism (otherwise known as sodomy), idolatry, alcoholism, drug pushing, and so on. Injustice is so institutionalized that when a certain class of people are thus victimized, whether fatally or any other way, it does not matter. But when it is the other way round, it is a slap to the nation and an attack on democracy.

The fact is that it is only the one who has the Spirit of God by being born again who desires and struggles to do good to please God. And unless we are born again, all our righteousness is like filthy rags in the sight of God (Isaiah 64:6). So it does not matter at all where anybody lives or comes from; it doesn't matter what color of skin one may have or one's country of residence. The Bible says that the heart of man is deceitful above all things, and desperately wicked (Jeremiah 17:9), and all wicked persons are doomed to perish eternally. But God sent the Redeemer/Savior into this world so that by believing in Him (Jesus Christ) and His finished work of salvation we shall be saved. Jesus Christ said, "For God so loved the world, that he gave his only begotten Son, that whosoever believeth in him should not perish, but have everlasting life. For God sent not his Son into the world to condemn the world; but that the world through him might be saved. He that believeth on him is not condemned: but he that believeth not is condemned already, because he hath not believed in the name of the only begotten Son of God" (John 3:16–18).

Unfortunately the world did not recognize Him (John 1:10), and many have continued to reject Him. But as many as have received Him, He gave to them the power or authority to become the sons (and daughters) of God, that is to them who believe in His name (John 1:12).

In times past, every young lady looked forward to that day when her right hand would be hooked to the left hand of a young man and they both would march down the aisle to the altar to be officially declared husband and wife. Almost every young man dreamed of the day when he would march a lady from the altar as well. That was the ideal situation! But all that is almost gone as men and women now choose other forms of family to build and other ways of starting their homes. We shall study God's ideal family structure versus the aberrations based on the scripture teaching and the effects of these aberrations on society.

Sociologists[1] and social anthropologists[2] believe and have

---

[1] Wikipedia defines *sociology* as "the scientific study of society, including patterns of social relationships, social interaction and culture." "Sociology," Wikipedia, last updated September 17, 2019, https://en.wikipedia.org/wiki/ Sociology.

[2] *Webster's All-in-One Dictionary and Thesaurus, 2008 Edition* defines *anthropology* as "the science of human beings." An online dictionary describes social anthropology as "the branch of anthropology that deals with cultural

proven that the family is the nucleus and strength of the society. So, if families are strong and healthy, the society is as well. And the converse is also true: if families are weak and unhealthy, then the society is also like that. This is why the devil continues to attack the family and the family structure, to ensure that families are in disarray, unhealthy, uncooperative, and contrary to God's plan for the standard family.

The major topics of *Family Structure by Choice* will be discussed under the following major headings:

- The Devil is against God and God's Work
- Marriage Was God's Idea
- Family Structures Today—Mankind's Creation
- Reasons for Avoidance of Marriage
- The Making of Single Parents
- The Ideal Family in God's View
- Effects of Single Parenting by Choice
- Conclusions and Recommendations

and social phenomena such as kinship systems or beliefs, especially of nonliterate peoples, societies, and cultures and their development" (http://www. wordreference.com/definition/social%20anthropology). September 17, 2019.

CHAPTER 2

THE DEVIL IS AGAINST GOD AND GOD'S WORK

EVERYTHING THAT GOD CREATED WAS GOOD, AT LEAST in His sight. He is perfect in all ways. After each day of creation, God looked at what He had created and saw that it was good. Seven times within the first chapter of the Bible, you read that it was good, as follows:

- "And God saw the light, that it was good: and God divided the light from the darkness" (Genesis 1:4).
- "And God called the dry land Earth; and the gathering together of the waters called he Seas: and God saw that it was good" (Genesis 1:10).

- "And the earth brought forth grass, and herb yielding seed after his kind, and the tree yielding fruit, whose seed was in itself, after his kind: and God saw that it was good" (Genesis 1:12).
- "And God made two great lights; the greater light to rule the day, and the lesser light to rule the night: he made the stars also. And God set them in the firmament of the heaven to give light upon the earth, And to rule over the day and over the night, and to divide the light from the darkness: and God saw that it was good" (Genesis 1:16–18).
- "And God created great whales, and every living creature that moveth, which the waters brought forth abundantly, after their kind, and every winged fowl after his kind: and God saw that it was good" (Genesis 1:21).
- "And God made the beast of the earth after his kind, and cattle after their kind, and every thing that creepeth upon the earth after his kind: and God saw that it was good" (Genesis 1:25).
- "And God saw every thing that he had made, and, behold, it was very good. And the evening and the morning were the sixth day" (Genesis 1:31).

The only thing that God saw as not good after creation was that man was alone, and God made a way immediately to correct the situation by making the woman. The Bible says, "And the Lord God said, It is not good that the man should be alone; I will make him an help meet for him" (Genesis 2:18).

Mankind was good and had fellowship with God until the visit and temptation by Satan, leading to the fall of mankind and their death spiritually and physically. The Bible says that it grieved God that He had created man. Read what the Bible says about this and what God decided to do as a result—to wipe out mankind:

> *And God saw that the wickedness of man was great in the earth, and that every imagination of the thoughts of his heart was only evil continually. And it repented the Lord that he had made man on the earth, and it grieved him at his heart. And the Lord said, I will destroy man whom I have created from the face of the earth; both man, and beast, and the creeping thing, and the fowls of the air; for it repenteth me that I have made them. (Genesis 6:5–7)*

The foregoing observation of God was also spoken and recorded by the prophet Jeremiah. He said that above all things, the heart of mankind is deceitful and desperately wicked, and he asked, "Who can know it?" (Jeremiah 17:9). As a result of the fall of mankind, we lost fellowship with God, who in turn cursed the ground (rather than human beings) for the sake of mankind, and subjected mankind to sweat and to live a life of sorrow.

> *And unto Adam he said, Because thou hast hearkened unto the voice of thy wife, and hast eaten of the tree, of which I commanded thee, saying, Thou shalt not eat of it: cursed is the ground for thy sake; in sorrow shalt thou eat of it all the days of thy life. (Genesis 3:17)*

In the same vein, God cursed the devil for his role in the fall and destruction of mankind, whom He had created in His image. The statement of God to that effect is as follows:

> *And the Lord God said unto the serpent, Because thou hast done this, thou art cursed above all cattle, and above every beast of the field; upon thy belly shalt thou go, and dust shalt thou eat all the days of thy life: And I will put enmity between thee and the woman, and between thy seed and her seed; it shall bruise thy head, and thou shalt bruise his heel. (Genesis 3:14–15)*

11

Human nature, therefore, became an enemy of God and remains so unless and until reconciled with God in Christ. Mankind may sometimes desire to please and obey God, but the evil nature in us keeps us from doing so.

> *Because the carnal mind is enmity against God: for it is not subject to the law of God, neither indeed can be. So then they that are in the flesh cannot please God. (Romans 8:7–8)*

For that which I do I allow not: for what I would, that do I not; but what I hate, that do I. If then I do that which I would not, I consent unto the law that it is good. Now then it is no more I that do it, but sin that dwelleth in me. For I know that in me (that is, in my flesh,) dwelleth no good thing: for to will is present with me; but how to perform that which is good I find not. For the good that I would I do not: but the evil which I would not, that I do. Now if I do that I would not, it is no more I that do it, but sin that dwelleth in me. I find then a law, that, when I would do good, evil is present with me. (Romans 7:15–21)

Being in enmity with God implies deadness in spirit, and the absence of and impossibility of fellowship with God. The apostle Paul refers to such people who are dead in spirit as people who were once alienated from God, hostile in mind, and doing evil deeds (Colossians 1:21 ESV). This scripture was addressed to the Colossians (and, of course, all gentiles as well as all human beings) who had become Christians.

Lucifer, who became the devil, was an archangel of God until he rebelled against God, and God expelled him from heaven.

> *How art thou fallen from heaven, O Lucifer, son of the morning! how art thou cut down to the ground, which didst weaken the nations! For thou hast said in thine heart, I will ascend into heaven, I will exalt my throne*

above the stars of God: I will sit also upon the mount of the congregation, in the sides of the north: I will ascend above the heights of the clouds; I will be like the most High. Yet thou shalt be brought down to hell, to the sides of the pit. (Isaiah 14:12–15)

By the multitude of thy merchandise they have filled the midst of thee with violence, and thou hast sinned: therefore I will cast thee as profane out of the mountain of God: and I will destroy thee, O covering cherub, from the midst of the stones of fire. Thine heart was lifted up because of thy beauty, thou hast corrupted thy wisdom by reason of thy brightness: I will cast thee to the ground, I will lay thee before kings, that they may behold thee. (Ezekiel 28:16–17)

God cast down Lucifer, along with the angels that supported him in his rebellion. They are doomed for hell, the place Jesus Christ said was prepared for them. Jesus said that He shall say also to them on the left hand who are cursed to depart from Him, into everlasting fire that is prepared for the devil and his angels (Matthew 25:41).

The devil has a three-fold agenda in this world, according to Jesus Christ. He said, "The thief cometh not, but for to steal, and to kill, and to destroy: I am come that they might have life, and that they might have it more abundantly" (John 10:10).

The apostle Peter further said "to be sober and be vigilant; because our adversary the devil walks about like a roaring lion, seeking people he may devour" (1 Peter 5:8). The devil accuses before God everyone who opposes him; hence he is described as the accuser of the brethren. In Revelation the Bible says, "And I heard a loud voice saying in heaven, Now is come salvation, and strength, and the kingdom of our God, and the power of his Christ: for the accuser of our brethren is cast down, which accused them before our God day and night" (Revelation 12:10).

The devil opposes God and desires that the plans of God, especially those for mankind, should fail by making mankind disobey or fail God, as found in the following passages:

> *Certain men, the children of Belial, are gone out from among you, and have withdrawn the inhabitants of their city, saying, Let us go and serve other gods, which ye have not known. (Deuteronomy 13:13)*

We read that Satan stood up against Israel and provoked David to number or take a census of the people of Israel (1 Chronicles 21:1).

> *And the Lord said unto Satan, Hast thou considered my servant Job, that there is none like him in the earth, a perfect and an upright man, one that feareth God, and escheweth evil? Then Satan answered the Lord, and said, Doth Job fear God for nought? Hast not thou made an hedge about him, and about his house, and about all that he hath on every side? thou hast blessed the work of his hands, and his substance is increased in the land. But put forth thine hand now, and touch all that he hath, and he will curse thee to thy face. (Job 1:8–11)*

> *Again there was a day when the sons of God came to present themselves before the Lord, and Satan came also among them to present himself before the Lord. And the Lord said unto Satan, From whence comest thou? And Satan answered the Lord, and said, From going to and fro in the earth, and from walking up and down in it.*

> *And the Lord said unto Satan, Hast thou considered my servant Job, that there is none like him in the earth, a perfect and an upright man, one that feareth God, and escheweth evil? and still he holdeth fast his integrity,*

although thou movedst me against him, to destroy him without cause.

And Satan answered the Lord, and said, Skin for skin, yea, all that a man hath will he give for his life. But put forth thine hand now, and touch his bone and his flesh, and he will curse thee to thy face. And the Lord said unto Satan, Behold, he is in thine hand; but save his life. So went Satan forth from the presence of the Lord, and smote Job with sore boils from the sole of his foot unto his crown. (Job 2:1–7)

But the prince of the kingdom of Persia withstood me one and twenty days: but, lo, Michael, one of the chief princes, came to help me; and I remained there with the kings of Persia. (Daniel 10:13)

And he shewed me Joshua the high priest standing before the angel of the Lord, and Satan standing at his right hand to resist him. And the Lord said unto Satan, The Lord rebuke thee, O Satan; even the Lord that hath chosen Jerusalem rebuke thee: is not this a brand plucked out of the fire? (Zechariah 3:1–2)

And he spake many things unto them in parables, saying, Behold, a sower went forth to sow; And when he sowed, some seeds fell by the way side, and the fowls came and devoured them up: Some fell upon stony places, where they had not much earth: and forthwith they sprung up, because they had no deepness of earth: And when the sun was up, they were scorched; and because they had no root, they withered away. And some fell among thorns; and the thorns sprung up, and choked them: But other fell into good ground, and brought forth fruit, some an hundredfold, some sixtyfold, some thirtyfold. Who hath ears to hear, let him hear. And the disciples came, and said unto him, Why speakest thou unto them in parables?

He answered and said unto them, Because it is given unto you to know the mysteries of the kingdom of heaven, but to them it is not given. For whosoever hath, to him shall be given, and he shall have more abundance: but whosoever hath not, from him shall be taken away even that he hath. Therefore speak I to them in parables: because they seeing see not; and hearing they hear not, neither do they understand. And in them is fulfilled the prophecy of Esaias, which saith, By hearing ye shall hear, and shall not understand; and seeing ye shall see, and shall not perceive: For this people's heart is waxed gross, and their ears are dull of hearing, and their eyes they have closed; lest at any time they should see with their eyes and hear with their ears, and should understand with their heart, and should be converted, and I should heal them.

But blessed are your eyes, for they see: and your ears, for they hear. For verily I say unto you, That many prophets and righteous men have desired to see those things which ye see, and have not seen them; and to hear those things which ye hear, and have not heard them. Hear ye therefore the parable of the sower. When any one heareth the word of the kingdom, and understandeth it not, then cometh the wicked one, and catcheth away that which was sown in his heart. This is he which received seed by the way side. (Matthew 13:3–19)

Jesus turned and addressed Peter as Satan and told Him to get thee behind Him: being a stumbling block to Him for reasons that he had in mind things that be not of God, but rather those that be of men (Matthew 16:23). Paul said that he had a great desire to see

16

the Thessalonians face-to-face, that he and his companions wanted to visit the Thessalonians once and again, but Satan hindered them (1 Thessalonians 2:18).

> *Fear none of those things which thou shalt suffer: behold, the devil shall cast some of you into prison, that ye may be tried; and ye shall have tribulation ten days: be thou faithful unto death, and I will give thee a crown of life. (Revelation 2:10)*

With the stance of the devil on the plans and works of God in view, it becomes easy to see that the devil hates to see the family stay together as God ordained it to be. Since the family is the nucleus of any society, good families would translate to good societies. And that is what the devil does not like or wish to see. Consequently the devil continues to work against the family to see that young people refuse to get married, as in Paul's letter to Timothy, and that married people get separated or divorced.[1] Paul said, "Now the Spirit speaketh expressly, that in the latter times some shall depart from the faith, giving heed to seducing spirits, and doctrines of devils; Speaking lies in hypocrisy; having their conscience seared with a hot iron; Forbidding to marry, and commanding to abstain from meats, which God hath created to be received with thanksgiving of them which believe and know the truth" (1 Timothy 4:1–3).

It is the will and arrangement of God for a man and a woman to be married and procreate. So the devil must persuade men and women to bear children out of wedlock. Unfortunately, people who cooperate with the devil in his opposition to God will also end with the devil in his final destination—hellfire—unless they repent

---

[1] Malachi 2:16 (NKJV) reads, "For the Lord God of Israel says That He hates divorce, For it covers one's garment with violence," Says the Lord of hosts. "Therefore take heed to your spirit, That you do not deal treacherously." Since God hates divorce (or "putting away" according to the King James Version), the devil must make people like divorce.

and put their trust in Jesus Christ, the Seed of the woman who, God proposed, would bruise the head of the devil. God said to the devil that He would put enmity between him and the woman, and between his seed and the woman's seed; her seed shall bruise Satan's head, and he shall bruise his heel (Genesis 3:15).

CHAPTER 3

MARRIAGE WAS GOD'S IDEA

THE IDEA OF FAMILY IS AS OLD AS MANKIND ON EARTH.
This information is based on the fact that God created man and woman (male and female) during the week of creation. The Bible says, "And God said, Let us make man in our image, after our likeness: and let them have dominion over the fish of the sea, and over the fowl of the air, and over the cattle, and over all the earth, and over every creeping thing that creepeth upon the earth. So God created man in his own image, in the image of God created he him; male and female created he them" (Genesis 1:26–27).

In God's infinite wisdom, for mankind to reproduce and be multiplied, there must be male and female in place. Initially God formed the male from dust, resulting in the man called Adam as per Genesis 2:7: "And the Lord God formed man of the dust of the ground, and breathed into his nostrils the breath of life; and man

19

became a living being." Similarly God formed all animals and birds from dust, and He observed that "it was not good for the man to be alone" and lonely (v. 18) in the garden into which God had placed him. Adam gave names to all the animals (v. 20), but he did not find any of them suitable for companionship. It sounds funny that these days some people prefer the company of cats, dogs, pigs, snakes, and other animals to a woman as wife, or a man as husband, or a child. Rather than form the woman from dust like the man and the animals and birds, in view of God's plan for mankind, He performed the first recorded surgical operation—He put Adam into a deep sleep, took out one of his ribs, and formed the rib into the woman.

The details of these accounts are as follows:

> *And the Lord God formed man of the dust of the ground, and breathed into his nostrils the breath of life; and man became a living soul. And the Lord God planted a garden eastward in Eden; and there he put the man whom he had formed.*
>
> *And the Lord God took the man, and put him into the Garden of Eden to dress it and to keep it. And the Lord God commanded the man, saying, Of every tree of the garden thou mayest freely eat: But of the tree of the knowledge of good and evil, thou shalt not eat of it: for in the day that thou eatest thereof thou shalt surely die. And the Lord God said, It is not good that the man should be alone; I will make him an help meet for him. And out of the ground the Lord God formed every beast of the field, and every fowl of the air; and brought them unto Adam to see what he would call them: and whatsoever Adam called every living creature, that was the name thereof. And Adam gave names to all cattle, and to the fowl of the air, and to every beast of the field; but for Adam there was not found an help meet for him. And the Lord God caused a deep sleep to fall upon Adam, and he slept: and*

he took one of his ribs, and closed up the flesh instead thereof;
And the rib, which the Lord God had taken from man, made he a
woman, and brought her unto the man. (Genesis 2:7–8, 15–22)

The reaction of Adam to the presentation of the woman to him by God was an expression of joy. The Bible says the Lord God made a woman of the rib, which He had taken from the man, and brought her to him. And Adam said that that was now bone of his bones, and flesh of his flesh; and that she should be called Woman, because she was taken out of Man (Genesis 2:22–23).

Thus the woman could be termed an extension of the man—a position that could be filled by neither another man nor an animal. God presented the woman, Eve, to Adam and by implication ruled that a man should therefore leave his father and mother and cleave to his wife, and the two of them shall become one flesh (husband and wife). "God blessed the man and his wife and ordered them to be fruitful, and multiply, and replenish the earth, and subdue it: and to have dominion over the fish of the sea, and over the birds of the air, and over every living thing that moves upon the earth" (Genesis 1:28).

The Bible records that the creation that God did "was very good" (Genesis 1:31). If the perfect God saw something and declared it very good, it would be ridiculous for imperfect human beings to fault it, or see it otherwise, or attempt to reverse it.

3.1 God Ordained Marriage

It was not a people, a nation, or a culture that originated marriage. God instituted it. He framed the structure and began the first family. The first family on record was that of Adam and Eve, the first man and first woman that God made. God had a purpose for marriage of man and woman, the result of which is the family. The family is the smallest unit and the nucleus of any society, and that is why it is very important to the study of a people, a church, or a nation. The family is dear to the heart of God as indicated in Malachi, to the extent that He rejected the people's offering for maltreating their wives.

> *And this have ye done again, covering the altar of the Lord with tears, with weeping, and with crying out, insomuch that he regardeth not the offering any more, or receiveth it with good will at your hand. Yet ye say, Wherefore? Because the Lord hath been witness between thee and the wife of thy youth, against whom thou hast dealt treacherously: yet is she thy companion, and the wife of thy covenant. And did not he make one? Yet had he the residue of the spirit. And wherefore one? That he might seek a godly seed. Therefore take heed to your spirit, and let none deal treacherously against the wife of his youth. (Malachi 2:13–15)*

The purposes of God in ordaining marriage include the following:

Love and Companionship

God said it is not good for the man to be alone (Genesis 2:18). God in His infinite wisdom and knowledge believed and said that it is not good for man to be alone. Human beings need a companion in whom to confide and share the special affection that is so personal and deep-rooted in the heart. Neither a bird, nor an animal, nor another man, nor children can fill the space for a woman in the heart and life of a man and vice versa. The Bible tells us that the foolishness of God is wiser than human beings and that the weakness of God is stronger than human beings (1 Corinthians 1:25). This accounts for the wrongness of homosexuality, bestiality, lesbianism, and singleness by choice other than for total dedication to the service of the Lord like John the Baptist.[1]

Procreation

Genesis 1:27–28 reads, "So God created man in his own image, in the image of God created he him; male and female created he them. And God blessed them, and God said unto them, Be fruitful, and multiply, and replenish the earth, and subdue it: and have dominion over the fish of the sea, and over the fowl of the air, and over every living thing that moveth upon the earth."

God proposed to fill the earth with the human race not by continuing to make additional people after Adam and Eve from dust. Rather God gave all His creatures the ability to replicate themselves from themselves. He also gave them the responsibility to do so in order to perpetuate their races and species. Some of the other instances of God commanding His creation to be fruitful and multiply are as follows:

> *And God created great whales, and every living creature that moveth, which the waters brought forth abundantly, after their kind, and every winged fowl after his kind: and God saw that it was good. And God blessed them, saying, Be fruitful, and multiply, and fill the waters*

---

[1] John was foreordained to be forerunner to Jesus Christ. He was to have a ministry *in the spirit of the (celibate) prophet Elijah.* Luke 1:13–17 reads, "But the angel said unto him, Fear not, Zacharias: for thy prayer is heard; and thy wife Elisabeth shall bear thee a son, and thou shalt call his name John. And thou shalt have joy and gladness; and many shall rejoice at his birth. For he shall be great in the sight of the Lord, and shall drink neither wine nor strong drink; and he shall be filled with the Holy Ghost, even from his mother's womb. And many of the children of Israel shall he turn to the Lord their God. And he shall go before him in the spirit and power of Elias, to turn the hearts of the fathers to the children, and the disobedient to the wisdom of the just; to make ready a people prepared for the Lord."

in the seas, and let fowl multiply in the earth. (Genesis 1:21–22)

Go forth of the ark, thou, and thy wife, and thy sons, and thy sons' wives with thee. Bring forth with thee every living thing that is with thee, of all flesh, both of fowl, and of cattle, and of every creeping thing that creepeth upon the earth; that they may breed abundantly in the earth, and be fruitful, and multiply upon the earth. (Genesis 8:16–17)

The flood that God released was to wipe out mankind and all creatures living on the surface of the earth as a result of humanity's sin, leaving out only Noah's family, which included men and women, together with a male and a female of every animal and bird as God ordered Noah to take into the ark. At the end of that flood, which left alive only Noah's family and the other creatures that Noah had taken into the ark, Noah offered God a sacrifice. Genesis 8:21–9:1 reads, "And the Lord smelled a sweet savour; and the Lord said in his heart, I will not again curse the ground any more for man's sake; for the imagination of man's heart is evil from his youth; neither will I again smite any more every thing living, as I have done. While the earth remaineth, seedtime and harvest, and cold and heat, and summer and winter, and day and night shall not cease. And God blessed Noah and his sons, and said unto them, Be fruitful, and multiply, and replenish the earth."

For Completeness

A stand-alone man or woman is incomplete until the man finds the bone of his bones and flesh of his flesh or until the woman finds the man whose removed rib she was created from and is united with him in marriage. The Bible references this idea as follows:

And the Lord God caused a deep sleep to fall upon Adam, and he slept: and he took one of his ribs, and closed up the flesh instead thereof; And the rib, which the Lord God had taken from man, made he a woman, and brought her unto the man. And Adam said, This is now bone of my bones, and flesh of my flesh: she shall be called Woman, because she was taken out of Man. Therefore shall a man leave his father and his mother, and shall cleave unto his wife: and they shall be one flesh. (Genesis 2:21–24)

This completeness also provides strength and warmth. The preacher says, "Two are better than one; because they have a good reward for their labour. For if they fall, the one will lift up his fellow: but woe to him that is alone when he falleth; for he hath not another to help him up. Again, if two lie together, then they have heat: but how can one be warm alone? And if one prevail against him, two shall withstand him; and a threefold cord is not quickly broken" (Ecclesiastes 4:9–12).

To Prevent Immorality

In 1 Corinthians 7:2–4 the Bible says, "Nevertheless, to avoid fornication, let every man have his own wife, and let every woman have her own husband. Let the husband render unto the wife due benevolence: and likewise also the wife unto the husband. The wife hath not power of her own body, but the husband: and likewise also the husband hath not power of his own body, but the wife."[2]

The flesh is quickly attracted to, and tempted by, the opposite sex. This accounts for the prevalence of sexual immorality all around in any and every society. Marriage is, therefore, the way that God has provided as an antidote, since sex is supposed to be free and readily available most often within any marriage, as is said in 1 Corinthians

---

[2] Note that the passage says *wife* and *husband*, not *girlfriend* and *boyfriend*.

7:4, above. This is provided so that each spouse practices self-control and godliness with contentment. The apostle Paul wrote, "But godliness with contentment is great gain" (1 Timothy 6:6).

To Typify the Union of Christ with the Church

God uses marriage to show what the relationship should be between Jesus Christ and His Church, which He loves so much that He died for her and keeps on caring for her.

> *For no man ever yet hated his own flesh; but nourisheth and cherisheth it, even as the Lord the church: for we are members of his body, of his flesh, and of his bones. For this cause shall a man leave his father and mother, and shall be joined unto his wife, and they two shall be one flesh. This is a great mystery: but I speak concerning Christ and the church. Nevertheless let every one of you in particular so love his wife even as himself; and the wife see that she reverence her husband. (Ephesians 5:29–33)*

For Providing a Firm Foundation for Society

God wants children to be brought up in homes that are conducive to developing a firm foundation for a godly society. "Charity begins at home" is a popular saying. But if the home is bereft of charity, then the children brought up in such a home have no charity (including discipline and godliness) to present or extend to society. Through the prophet Malachi, the Word of God says, "Did he not make them one, with a portion of the Spirit in their union? And what was the one God seeking? Godly offspring. So guard yourselves in your spirit, and let none of you be faithless to the wife of your youth" (Malachi 2:15 ESV).

3.2 Marriage After The Fall Of Mankind

The Bible says that the woman was presented to the man and that he and his wife were both naked and not ashamed. It should be noted that in the first three chapters of Genesis—before and immediately after the temptation and fall of humankind described in Genesis 3:1–19—all references are to *the man and his wife* (i.e., one man and his only wife).

The Temptation and Fall of Mankind
Now the serpent was more subtil than any beast of the field which the Lord God had made. And he said unto the woman, Yea, hath God said, Ye shall not eat of every tree of the garden? And the woman said unto the serpent, We may eat of the fruit of the trees of the garden: But of the fruit of the tree which is in the midst of the garden, God hath said, Ye shall not eat of it, neither shall ye touch it, lest ye die.

And the serpent said unto the woman, Ye shall not surely die: For God doth know that in the day ye eat thereof, then your eyes shall be opened, and ye shall be as gods, knowing good and evil. And when the woman saw that the tree was good for food, and that it was pleasant to the eyes, and a tree to be desired to make one wise, she took of the fruit thereof, and did eat, and gave also unto her husband with her; and he did eat. And the eyes of them both were opened, and they knew that they were naked; and they sewed fig leaves together, and made themselves aprons.

And they heard the voice of the Lord God walking in the garden in the cool of the day: and Adam and his wife hid themselves from the presence of the Lord God amongst the

27

trees of the garden. And the Lord God called unto Adam, and said unto him, Where art thou? And he said, I heard thy voice in the garden, and I was afraid, because I was naked; and I hid myself.

And he said, Who told thee that thou wast naked? Hast thou eaten of the tree, whereof I commanded thee that thou shouldest not eat? And the man said, The woman whom thou gavest to be with me, she gave me of the tree, and I did eat. And the Lord God said unto the woman, What is this that thou hast done? And the woman said, The serpent beguiled me, and I did eat. And the Lord God said unto the serpent, Because thou hast done this, thou art cursed above all cattle, and above every beast of the field; upon thy belly shalt thou go, and dust shalt thou eat all the days of thy life: And I will put enmity between thee and the woman, and between thy seed and her seed; it shall bruise thy head, and thou shalt bruise his heel.

Unto the woman he said, I will greatly multiply thy sorrow and thy conception; in sorrow thou shalt bring forth children; and thy desire shall be to thy husband, and he shall rule over thee. And unto Adam he said, Because thou hast hearkened unto the voice of thy wife, and hast eaten of the tree, of which I commanded thee, saying, Thou shalt not eat of it: cursed is the ground for thy sake; in sorrow shalt thou eat of it all the days of thy life; Thorns also and thistles shall it bring forth to thee; and thou shalt eat the herb of the field; In the sweat of thy face shalt thou eat bread, till thou return unto the ground; for out of it wast thou taken: for dust thou art, and unto dust shalt thou return. (Genesis 3:1–19)

Up till this time, it appeared that there was still order in creation. Also in Genesis 4:1 the Bible says that Adam knew Eve his wife, and she conceived, and gave birth to Cain, and said that from the Lord she had gotten a man.

The first occurrence of polygamy in the Bible was that of Lamech: "And Lamech took unto him two wives: the name of the one was Adah, and the name of the other Zillah" (Genesis 4:19). Lamech married two wives. And many of the popular men in the Old Testament were polygamous. It appears that God allowed them to do so (perhaps in His permissive will).[3] This is one of the instances that reveals that God gives human beings free will to choose. Examples of biblical celebrities who were polygamous are Abraham, Esau, Jacob, Elkanah, David, and Solomon. However, Jesus Christ taught that God's ideal and perfect will for marriage is monogamy. "And [Jesus] answered and said unto them, Have ye not read, that he which made them at the beginning made them male and female, and said, For this cause shall a man leave father and mother, and shall cleave to his wife: and they twain shall be one flesh?" (Matthew 19:4–5).

3.2.1   Instances of Divorce in The Bible

There does not appear to be any single explicit instance of divorce in the Bible other than the case of the general divorce of foreign wives on religious/legal grounds after the return of the exiles from Babylon.

> *Now when Ezra had prayed, and when he had confessed, weeping and casting himself down before the house of God, there assembled unto him out of Israel a very great*

---

[3] The permissive will of God does not imply God's approval or sanction of sin or evil. It just means that God does not intervene directly to keep it from occurring. God's perfect will is stated in Romans 12:2 thus: "*And be not conformed to this world*: but be ye transformed by the renewing of your mind, that ye may prove what *is* that good, and acceptable, and perfect, will of God" (emphasis added).

> *congregation of men and women and children: for the*
> *people wept very sore. And Shechaniah the son of Jehiel,*
> *one of the sons of Elam, answered and said unto Ezra,*
> *We have trespassed against our God, and have taken*
> *strange wives of the people of the land: yet now there is*
> *hope in Israel concerning this thing.*

Now therefore let us make a covenant with our God to put away all the wives, and such as are born of them, according to the counsel of my lord, and of those that tremble at the commandment of our God; and let it be done according to the law. Arise; for this matter belongeth unto thee: we also will be with thee: be of good courage, and do it. Then arose Ezra, and made the chief priests, the Levites, and all Israel, to swear that they should do according to this word. And they sware. (Ezra 10:1–5)

3.2.2 Instances of Polyandry in The Bible

Explicitly there are no instances of polyandry—a woman married to more than one man at the same time. However, even though in the case of adultery the couple may not be living together under one roof, adultery could be seen in light of polyandry since the Bible says that you become one with a prostitute with whom you have sex. The passage reads, "What? know ye not that he which is joined to an harlot is one body? for two, saith he, shall be one flesh" (1 Corinthians 6:16). For this reason, the following laws in the Old Testament prohibit polyandry:

> *And the man that committeth adultery with another*
> *man's wife, even he that committeth adultery with his*
> *neighbour's wife, the adulterer and the adulteress shall*
> *surely be put to death. (Leviticus 20:10)*
> *If a man be found lying with a woman married to an*
> *husband, then they shall both of them die, both the man*

that lay with the woman, and the woman: so shalt thou
put away evil from Israel. (Deuteronomy 22:22)

3.2.3   Unmarried (or Single) Mothers

Unmarried (or single) mothers were not known or popular in the Old Testament, because such persons would be classified harlots or whores, and nobody would want to be so stigmatized. A harlot, also known as a prostitute or whore, is a woman who engages in sex or "sells" herself via sexual activity for financial gain or favor. Put another way, a harlot is a woman whose merchandise is sex. Men in Old Testament times were not known to be prostitutes generally, except in relation to the worship of some gods such as the Canaanite god Asherah: "He also tore down the quarters of the male shrine prostitutes that were in the temple of the Lord, the quarters where women did weaving for Asherah" (2 Kings 23:7 NIV). And 1 Kings 14:24 says that there were also male cult prostitutes in the land. They practiced all the abominable acts of the nations that the Lord drove out of the land in favor of the Israelites.

In view of the derogation of this class of women, there are many warnings, counsels, and rules against harlotry in the Old Testament, some of which are stated below:

Do not prostitute thy daughter, to cause her to be a
whore; lest the land fall to whoredom, and the land
become full of wickedness. (Leviticus 19:29)

If any man take a wife, and go in unto her, and hate her,
And give occasions of speech against her, and bring up an
evil name upon her, and say, I took this woman, and
when I came to her, I found her not a maid: Then shall
the father of the damsel, and her mother, take and bring
forth the tokens of the damsel's virginity unto the elders of
the city in the gate: And the damsel's father shall say unto
the elders, I gave my daughter unto this man to wife, and

he hateth her; And, lo, he hath given occasions of speech against her, saying, I found not thy daughter a maid; and yet these are the tokens of my daughter's virginity. And they shall spread the cloth before the elders of the city. And the elders of that city shall take that man and chastise him; And they shall amerce him in an hundred shekels of silver, and give them unto the father of the damsel, because he hath brought up an evil name upon a virgin of Israel: and she shall be his wife; he may not put her away all his days. But if this thing be true, and the tokens of virginity be not found for the damsel: Then they shall bring out the damsel to the door of her father's house, and the men of her city shall stone her with stones that she die: because she hath wrought folly in Israel, to play the whore in her father's house: so shalt thou put evil away from among you. (Deuteronomy 22:13–21)

There shall be no whore of the daughters of Israel, nor a sodomite of the sons of Israel. Thou shalt not bring the hire of a whore, or the price of a dog, into the house of the Lord thy God for any vow: for even both these are abomination unto the Lord thy God. (Deuteronomy 23:17–18)

Now Jephthah the Gileadite was a mighty man of valor, but he was the son of a harlot; and Gilead begot Jephthah. (Judges 11:1 NKJV)

For the purpose of the story of the actions of Jephthah, it was enough to state that he was a mighty man of valor. However, the passage goes on to add a stigma on him, which begins with the conjunction *but*, after which it is said that his mother was a harlot. This indicates that it was a shameful thing to be associated with, or related to, a harlot. Effectively Jephthah's mother appears to be the only unmarried mother mentioned in the Old Testament apart from

32

the two prostitutes who claimed motherhood of a living child in the early days of Solomon's kingship.[4]

Proverbs 2:16 says, "Wisdom will save you from the immoral woman, from the seductive words of the promiscuous woman" (NLT).

> *For the lips of a strange woman drop as an honeycomb, and her mouth is smoother than oil: But her end is bitter as wormwood, sharp as a two-edged sword. Her feet go down to death; her steps take hold on hell. Lest thou shouldest ponder the path of life, her ways are moveable, that thou canst not know them. Hear me now therefore, O ye children, and depart not from the words of my mouth. Remove thy way far from her, and come not nigh the door of her house: Lest thou give thine honour unto others, and thy years unto the cruel: Lest strangers be filled with thy wealth; and thy labours be in the house of a stranger; And thou mourn at the last, when thy flesh and thy body are consumed, And say, How have I hated instruction, and my heart despised reproof; And have not obeyed the voice of my teachers, nor inclined mine ear to them that instructed me!*

---

[4] We read in 1 Kings 3:16–22, "Then came there two women, that were harlots, unto the king, and stood before him. And the one woman said, O my lord, I and this woman dwell in one house; and I was delivered of a child with her in the house. And it came to pass the third day after that I was delivered, that this woman was delivered also: and we were together; there was no stranger with us in the house, save we two in the house. And this woman's child died in the night; because she overlaid it. And she arose at midnight, and took my son from beside me, while thine handmaid slept, and laid it in her bosom, and laid her dead child in my bosom. And when I rose in the morning to give my child suck, behold, it was dead: but when I had considered it in the morning, behold, it was not my son, which I did bear. And the other woman said, Nay; but the living is my son, and the dead is thy son. And this said, No; but the dead is thy son, and the living is my son. Thus they spake before the king."

I was almost in all evil in the midst of the congregation and assembly. Drink waters out of thine own cistern, and running waters out of thine own well. Let thy fountains be dispersed abroad, and rivers of waters in the streets. Let them be only thine own, and not strangers' with thee. Let thy fountain be blessed: and rejoice with the wife of thy youth. Let her be as the loving hind and pleasant roe; let her breasts satisfy thee at all times; and be thou ravished always with her love. And why wilt thou, my son, be ravished with a strange woman, and embrace the bosom of a stranger? (Proverbs 5:3–20)

For she sitteth at the door of her house, on a seat in the high places of the city, To call passengers who go right on their ways: Whoso is simple, let him turn in hither: and as for him that wanteth understanding, she saith to him, Stolen waters are sweet, and bread eaten in secret is pleasant. But he knoweth not that the dead are there; and that her guests are in the depths of hell. (Proverbs 9:14–18)

Proverbs 29:3 reads, "Whoso loveth wisdom rejoiceth his father: but he that keepeth company with harlots spendeth his substance." In many passages in the Bible and from the mouths of many prophets, God used the lifestyle of a harlot to typify the waywardness of Israel, straying from Him to other gods.

Isaiah 1:21 reads, "How is the faithful city become an harlot! it was full of judgment; righteousness lodged in it; but now murderers." Further in the book of Isaiah we read the following:

But draw near hither, ye sons of the sorceress, the seed of the adulterer and the whore. Upon a lofty and high mountain hast thou set thy bed: even thither wentest thou up to offer sacrifice. Behind the doors also and the posts hast thou set up thy remembrance: for thou hast discovered thyself to another than me, and art gone up; thou hast enlarged thy bed, and made thee a covenant with them; thou lovedst their bed where thou sawest it. And thou wentest to the king with ointment, and didst increase thy perfumes, and didst send thy messengers far off, and didst debase thyself even unto hell. (Isaiah 57:3, 7–9)

Also consider the following scriptures:

- "Therefore the showers have been withholden, and there hath been no latter rain; and thou hadst a whore's forehead, thou refusedst to be ashamed" (Jeremiah 3:3).
- "And Aholah played the harlot when she was mine; and she doted on her lovers, on the Assyrians her neighbours" (Ezekiel 23:5).
- "The beginning of the word of the Lord by Hosea. And the Lord said to Hosea, Go, take unto thee a wife of whoredoms and children of whoredoms: for the land hath committed great whoredom, departing from the Lord" (Hosea 1:2).
- "For their mother hath played the harlot: she that conceived them hath done shamefully: for she said, I will go after my lovers, that give me my bread and my water, my wool and my flax, mine oil and my drink" (Hosea 2:5).
- "My people ask counsel at their stocks, and their staff declareth unto them: for the spirit of whoredoms hath caused them to err, and they have gone a whoring from under their God" (Hosea 4:12).
- "And all the graven images thereof shall be beaten to pieces, and all the hires thereof shall be burned with the fire, and all the idols thereof will I lay desolate: for she gathered it of the hire of an harlot, and they shall return to the hire of an harlot" (Micah 1:7).

3.2.4 Widowed Fathers and Widowed Mothers

This is another group of parents who arise from the death of one spouse. This is an uncontrollable situation. It also gives rise to levirate marriage, which was also permitted/mandated by the Old Testament. Levirate marriage was a custom that required a man to marry the widow of his brother. The law regarding levirate marriage is as follows:

> *If brethren dwell together, and one of them die, and have no child, the wife of the dead shall not marry without unto a stranger: her husband's brother shall go in unto her, and take her to him to wife, and perform the duty of an husband's brother unto her. And it shall be, that the firstborn which she beareth shall succeed in the name of his brother which is dead, that his name be not put out of Israel.*

> *And if the man like not to take his brother's wife, then let his brother's wife go up to the gate unto the elders, and say, My husband's brother refuseth to raise up unto his brother a name in Israel, he will not perform the duty of my husband's brother. Then the elders of his city shall call him, and speak unto him: and if he stand to it, and say, I like not to take her; Then shall his brother's wife come unto him in the presence of the elders, and loose his shoe from off his foot, and spit in his face, and shall answer and say, So shall it be done unto that man that will not build up his brother's house. And his name shall be called in Israel, The house of him that hath his shoe loosed. (Deuteronomy 25:5–10)*

The case of Boaz and Ruth appears to be a good example of this marriage, notwithstanding that Boaz was not a brother of Ruth's late husband but a close relative. The story is as follows:

Now this was the manner in former time in Israel concerning redeeming and concerning changing, for to confirm all things; a man plucked off his shoe, and gave it to his neighbour: and this was a testimony in Israel. Therefore the kinsman said unto Boaz, Buy it for thee. So he drew off his shoe. And Boaz said unto the elders, and unto all the people, Ye are witnesses this day, that I have bought all that was Elimelech's, and all that was Chilion's and Mahlon's, of the hand of Naomi. Moreover Ruth the Moabitess, the wife of Mahlon, have I purchased to be my wife, to raise up the name of the dead upon his inheritance, that the name of the dead be not cut off from among his brethren, and from the gate of his place: ye are witnesses this day. And all the people that were in the gate, and the elders, said, We are witnesses. The Lord make the woman that is come into thine house like Rachel and like Leah, which two did build the house of Israel: and do thou worthily in Ephratah, and be famous in Bethlehem:

And let thy house be like the house of Pharez, whom Tamar bare unto Judah, of the seed which the Lord shall give thee of this young woman. So Boaz took Ruth, and she was his wife: and when he went in unto her, the Lord gave her conception, and she bare a son. And the women said unto Naomi, Blessed be the Lord, which hath not left thee this day without a kinsman, that his name may be famous in Israel. And he shall be unto thee a restorer of thy life, and a nourisher of thine old age: for thy daughter in law, which loveth thee, which is better to thee than seven sons, hath born him. And Naomi took the child, and laid it in her bosom, and became nurse unto it. And the women her neighbours gave it a name, saying, There is a son born to Naomi; and they called his

*name Obed: he is the father of Jesse, the father of David.
(Ruth 4:7–17)*

On the other hand, the punishment that God meted out to the sons of Judah for refusing to perform this duty to their late brother's widow is an indication of how important the practice of levirate marriage was in the sight of God:

> *And Judah took a wife for Er his firstborn, whose name was Tamar. And Er, Judah's firstborn, was wicked in the sight of the Lord; and the Lord slew him. And Judah said unto Onan, Go in unto thy brother's wife, and marry her, and raise up seed to thy brother. And Onan knew that the seed should not be his; and it came to pass, when he went in unto his brother's wife, that he spilled it on the ground, lest that he should give seed to his brother. And the thing which he did displeased the Lord: wherefore he slew him also. (Genesis 38:6–10)*

Generally, levirate marriage has become unpopular, especially because most widowed women want to choose by themselves the men they wish to relate with. And in most cases such men do not belong to the family of the late husbands.

3.2.5 Single Parenting by Choice

In recent times, single parenting by choice has become popular in Europe and the United States. This is a phenomenon whereby a man "engages the services" of a woman to bear a child for him without any commitment to marriage. You hear a man introduce a woman who has children for him as his girlfriend or as the mother of his kid(s). In the same manner a woman refuses marriage but engages some man or men to give her babies, whom she wants to own to the exclusion of the man as father. In this case the woman most often obtains legal restraint limiting the man's access to the children such that she should not even have opportunities to introduce him as the father of her children.

This phenomenon gained more ground with the pressure placed on society by feminism and the women's liberation movement, which was focused on equal rights of women and which has gradually eroded the authority and respect of many a man in the family and society.

CHAPTER 4

FAMILY STRUCTURES TODAY—MANKIND'S CREATION

AS AN EXTENSION OF MANKIND'S DISOBEDIENCE TO God (sin), humanity has deviated from God's ideal marriage structure as discussed in chapter 7, to come. Usually the unregenerate man prefers doing things that God has said not to do, and not to do what God wants done. However, the regenerate man oftentimes finds himself struggling in his spirit. In fact, the apostle Paul beautifully presented this issue in his epistle to the Romans thus:

For I know that in me (that is, in my flesh,) dwelleth no good thing: for to will is present with me; but how to perform that which is good I find not. For the good that I would I do not: but the evil which I would not, that I do. Now if I do that I would not, it is no more I that do it, but sin that dwelleth in me. I find then a law, that, when I would do good, evil is present with me. For I delight in the law of God after the inward man: But I see another law in my members, warring against the law of my mind, and bringing me into captivity to the law of sin which is in my members. O wretched man that I am! who shall deliver me from the body of this death? I thank God through Jesus Christ our Lord. So then with the mind I myself serve the law of God; but with the flesh the law of sin. (Romans 7:18–25)

This disobedience to God manifests vividly in the structures of family that abound these days—mostly an aberration of the original. We shall consider here six such structures:

- polygamy
- polyandry
- gay family or same-sex marriage
- single-parent family
- cohabitation
- two-parent family with blurred parental roles

4.1 Polygamy

Polygamy has been defined as "the practice of having more than one wife or husband at one time."[1] It is the type of marriage in which a man (usually) is married to more than one woman at a time. *Poly*, opposite of *mono*, has its root in the Greek word πολύς (*polús*, meaning "many, much"). Polygamy is a family structure that, as seen earlier, was practiced in Old Testament times and was not condemned explicitly by God *probably* because He wanted to fill the earth in line with His command to mankind after creation and after the flood that left only Noah and his family in the world. "He blessed them and told them to be fruitful, and multiply, and replenish the earth, and subdue it: God asked them to have dominion over the fish

---

[1] *Webster's All-in-One Dictionary and Thesaurus*, (2008 edition), s.v. "polygamy."

of the sea, and over the birds of the air, and over every living thing that moves on the earth" (Genesis 1:28). Similarly, "God blessed Noah and his sons, and told them to be fruitful, and multiply, and replenish the earth" (Genesis 9:1).

In most cases polygamy arises from lack of contentment, where a man is not satisfied with the wife or wives he already has. It is hardly due to unavoidable circumstances, as in the case of levirate marriage.[2] An instance of levirate marriage was when Judah instructed his son Onan to take up his late brother's widow (see Genesis 38:8): "And Judah said unto Onan, Go in unto thy brother's wife, and marry her, and raise up seed to thy brother."

Polygamy is a status symbol in some cultures. In such cases a man's wealth is measured by a combination of the number of wives and children he has and the other forms of property he owns. However, Jesus Christ explained that polygamy was not in the original plan of God: "And he answered and said unto them, Have ye not read, that he which made them at the beginning made them

---

[2] Levirate marriage is the kind of marriage where a man marries the widow of his late brother in order to care for her and have children, some of whom should bear the name of the late brother, especially if the man died before having any children. This requirement is specified in Deuteronomy as follows: "If brethren dwell together, and one of them die, and have no child, the wife of the dead shall not marry without unto a stranger: her husband's brother shall go in unto her, and take her to him to wife, and perform the duty of an husband's brother unto her. And it shall be, that the firstborn which she beareth shall succeed in the name of his brother which is dead, that his name be not put out of Israel. And if the man like not to take his brother's wife, then let his brother's wife go up to the gate unto the elders, and say, My husband's brother refuseth to raise up unto his brother a name in Israel, he will not perform the duty of my husband's brother. Then the elders of his city shall call him, and speak unto him: and if he stand to it, and say, I like not to take her; Then shall his brother's wife come unto him in the presence of the elders, and loose his shoe from off his foot, and spit in his face, and shall answer and say, So shall it be done unto that man that will not build up his brother's house. And his name shall be called in Israel, The house of him that hath his shoe loosed" (Deuteronomy 25:5–10).

male and female, And said, For this cause shall a man leave father and mother, and shall cleave to his wife: and they twain shall be one flesh?" (Matthew 19:4–5).

It should be noted, however, that some religions such as Islam encourage men to marry many wives. A man is allowed to marry up to a total of four[3] provided he loves all the women equally—an impossibility by all standards. Also Mormonism calls polygamy "plural marriage," and the leaders of the Church of Jesus Christ of Latter-day Saints publicly practiced it in the nineteenth century. As many as 30 percent of the membership of the religion also practiced it. Polygamy was instituted by the founder, Joseph Smith, in the 1830s and then publicly practiced from 1852 to 1890.[4] The practice was, however, officially discontinued in 1904 when the president of the church, "Joseph F. Smith disavowed polygamy before [the US] Congress."

One of the major reasons for encouraging polygamy by these and other religions is most likely for propagation of the faith—to rapidly multiply the population of their members. Having many children, who are supposed to automatically take up their father's faith, should facilitate the growth of the populations of the adherents of that faith. And since having many children was also one of the indices for measuring wealth, and given that there is a limit to the number of children a woman can safely bear, only one wife would scuttle the idea. It was also advantageous to have many children especially in some cultures where the economy was mainly agrarian and most men were mainly farmers who needed many hands on the farm.

Unfortunately such polygamous families are fraught with competition and rivalry among the wives and between the children. Illiteracy and hatred, as well as suspicion, are common features in

---

[3] "Polygyny in Islam," Wikipedia, last updated December 22, 2017, https://en.wikipedia.org/wiki/Polygyny_in_Islam.

[4] "Mormonism and Polygamy," Wikipedia, last updated December 22, 2017, https://en.wikipedia.org/wiki/Mormonism_and_polygamy.

such families. Much of these problems arise from the fact that the father of the home allocates his resources to the children according to the magnitude of love he has for their respective mothers. In effect, the children of the most loved wife receive a higher allocation of resources, and so it goes in order down to the least loved wife. Meanwhile, the man's resources are not limitless. Other negative characteristics of polygamy include jealousy, envy, secrecy, and murder.

Even though God loved King David, whom God described as a man after His own heart,[5] most of the aforementioned ills mentioned, accompanied by rape, incest, and rebellion, were found in his polygamous family.

Another negative is the difficulty in, or even the impossibility of, having a family that is culturally and religiously in total harmony. An example from the life of King Solomon speaks volumes here. Scriptures say that King Solomon had seven hundred wives (princesses of other nations) and three hundred concubines, and his wives turned away his heart (1 Kings 11:3). Each wife went into the marriage with the god or goddess (and most likely the culture) of her people. Consequently Solomon had to build a shrine for each wife's god or goddess in order to please every one of them. With all the gods in the domain of Solomon, he became idolatrous and could not discourage idolatry in his kingdom.

First Kings 11:1–9 reads as follows:

> *But king Solomon loved many strange women, together with the daughter of Pharaoh, women of the Moabites, Ammonites, Edomites, Zidonians, and Hittites: Of the nations concerning which the Lord said unto the children of Israel, Ye shall not go in to them, neither shall they*

---

[5] Acts 13:22: "And when he had removed him, he raised up unto them David to be their king; to whom also he gave their testimony, and said, I have found David the son of Jesse, a man after mine own heart, which shall fulfil all my will."

come in unto you: for surely they will turn away your heart after their gods: Solomon clave unto these in love. And he had seven hundred wives, princesses, and three hundred concubines: and his wives turned away his heart.

For it came to pass, when Solomon was old, that his wives turned away his heart after other gods: and his heart was not perfect with the Lord his God, as was the heart of David his father. For Solomon went after Ashtoreth the goddess of the Zidonians, and after Milcom the abomination of the Ammonites. And Solomon did evil in the sight of the Lord, and went not fully after the Lord, as did David his father.

Then did Solomon build an high place for Chemosh, the abomination of Moab, in the hill that is before Jerusalem, and for Molech, the abomination of the children of Ammon. And likewise did he for all his strange wives, which burnt incense and sacrificed unto their gods. And the Lord was angry with Solomon, because his heart was turned from the Lord God of Israel, which had appeared unto him twice.

4.2 Polyandry

I have never seen, but only read about, this family structure whereby one woman is legitimately married to more than one husband at a time. Under normal circumstances in real life, it is only a prostitute that makes herself available to more than one man for sexual intercourse; and in scripture prostitution is prohibited: "There shall be no whore of the daughters of Israel, nor a sodomite of the sons of Israel" (Deuteronomy 23:17). However, it is said that the two best locations where polyandry is practiced even into this twenty-first century "are the Plateau of Tibet (a region shared by

46

India, Nepal, and the Tibet Autonomous Region of China) and the Marquesas Islands in the South Pacific." *Encyclopedia Britannica* claims, "Polyandry is generally a response to peculiar localized conditions such as sex (gender) ratios, adult male mortality, male absenteeism, social stratification, and the group's economic basis."[6] Whatever excuses may be advanced for the existence of this phenomenon, which appears good to those who practice it, in view of the scriptures, it is an aberration. No mention of polyandry appears in the Bible, perhaps because it was not a common practice. An article, "Why Is Polyandry Prohibited in Islam?" gives five reasons and closes with, "These reasons may clearly show why polyandry is uncommon and frowned upon among Muslims and most people in the world. The Islamic point of view on this issue, however, can be summarized as: 'Allah desires ease for you, and He does not desire hardship for you' (2:185), and Allah knows best what is good for you."[7]

4.3 Gay Family or Same-Sex Marriage

Just as the name implies, this is the marriage of a man to another man or of a woman to another woman. Another term for same-sex attraction is *gay*, which is a synonym for *homosexual*. Homosexual women are known as lesbians, and lesbianism appears not to be as old as male homosexuality. All references to homosexuality in the Bible seem to focus on men only. The people of Sodom and Gomorrah who practiced homosexuality were men. The people went and asked Lot where *the men* were who came in to him that night. "They said he should bring them out to them so that they might have carnal knowledge of them" (Genesis 19:5).

Over the centuries, homosexuality has been practiced secretly

---

[6] "Polyandry," *Encyclopædia Britannica*, last updated September 18, 2017, www.britannica.com/topic/polyandry-marriage.

[7] "Why Is Polyandry Prohibited in Islam?" Salam Islam, accessed January 29, 2018, https://salamislam.com/content/why-polyandry-prohibited-islam/3.

all over the world, apart from the places where it is known to have occurred, Sodom and Gomorrah, the former from where the word *sodomy* is derived—cities that God destroyed with fire and brimstone. The details of this story are recorded in Genesis 19:1–25:

> *And there came two angels to Sodom at even; and Lot sat in the gate of Sodom: and Lot seeing them rose up to meet them; and he bowed himself with his face toward the ground; And he said, Behold now, my lords, turn in, I pray you, into your servant's house, and tarry all night, and wash your feet, and ye shall rise up early, and go on your ways. And they said, Nay; but we will abide in the street all night. And he pressed upon them greatly; and they turned in unto him, and entered into his house; and he made them a feast, and did bake unleavened bread, and they did eat.*
>
> *But before they lay down, the men of the city, even the men of Sodom, compassed the house round, both old and young, all the people from every quarter: And they called unto Lot, and said unto him, Where are the men which came in to thee this night? bring them out unto us, that we may know them.*
>
> *And Lot went out at the door unto them, and shut the door after him, And said, I pray you, brethren, do not so wickedly. Behold now, I have two daughters which have not known man; let me, I pray you, bring them out unto you, and do ye to them as is good in your eyes: only unto these men do nothing; ... And he said unto him, See, I have accepted thee concerning this thing also, that I will not overthrow this city, for the which thou hast spoken. Haste thee, escape thither; for I cannot do anything till thou be come thither. Therefore the name of the city was called Zoar. The sun was risen upon the earth when Lot*

*entered into Zoar. Then the Lord rained upon Sodom
and upon Gomorrah brimstone and fire from the Lord
out of heaven; And he overthrew those cities, and all
the plain, and all the inhabitants of the cities, and that
which grew upon the ground.*

The Bible calls homosexuality a wicked and vile act in Genesis
19:6–7 (above). Romans 1:26–27 has this to say about it: "For this
cause God gave them up unto vile affections: for even their women
did change the natural use into that which is against nature: And
likewise also the men, leaving the natural use of the woman, burned in
their lust one toward another; men with men working that which is
unseemly, and receiving in themselves that recompence of their error
which was meet."

And God outlawed homosexuality in Israel, His intended ideal
nation: "Thou shalt not lie with mankind, as with womankind: it is
abomination" (Leviticus 18:22).

There are several other passages in scripture in which gay
relationships are exposed or condemned. Some of these passages

are as follows:

> *So God created man in his own image, in the image of
> God created he him; male and female created he them.
> (Genesis 1:27)*

> *Male and female created he them; and blessed them,
> and called their name Adam, in the day when they were
> created. (Genesis 5:2)*

> *If a man also lie with mankind, as he lieth with a
> woman, both of them have committed an abomination:
> they shall surely be put to death; their blood shall be upon
> them. (Leviticus 20:13)*

There shall be no whore of the daughters of Israel, nor a sodomite of the sons of Israel. (Deuteronomy 23:17)

Now as they were making their hearts merry, behold, the men of the city, certain sons of Belial, beset the house round about, and beat at the door, and spake to the master of the house, the old man, saying, Bring forth the man that came into thine house, that we may know him. And the man, the master of the house, went out unto them, and said unto them, Nay, my brethren, nay, I pray you, do not so wickedly; seeing that this man is come into mine house, do not this folly. Behold, here is my daughter a maiden, and his concubine; them I will bring out now, and humble ye them, and do with them what seemeth good unto you: but unto this man do not so vile a thing. (Judges 19:22–24)

And Judah did evil in the sight of the Lord, and they provoked him to jealousy with their sins which they had committed, above all that their fathers had done. For they also built them high places, and images, and groves, on every high hill, and under every green tree. And there were also sodomites in the land: and they did according to all the abominations of the nations which the Lord cast out before the children of Israel. (1 Kings 14:22–24)

And Asa did that which was right in the eyes of the Lord, as did David his father. And he took away the sodomites out of the land, and removed all the idols that his fathers had made. And also Maachah his mother, even her he removed from being queen, because she had made an idol in a grove; and Asa destroyed her idol, and burnt it by the brook Kidron. (1 Kings 15:11–13)

And he walked in all the ways of Asa his father; he turned not aside from it, doing that which was right in the eyes of the Lord: nevertheless the high places were not taken away; for the people offered and burnt incense yet in the high places. ... And the remnant of the sodomites, which remained in the days of his father Asa, he took out of the land. (1 Kings 22:43, 46)

The shew of their countenance doth witness against them; and they declare their sin as Sodom, they hide it not. Woe unto their soul! for they have rewarded evil unto themselves. Say ye to the righteous, that it shall be well with him: for they shall eat the fruit of their doings. Woe unto the wicked! it shall be ill with him: for the reward of his hands shall be given him. (Isaiah 3:9–11)

Behold, this was the iniquity of thy sister Sodom, pride, fulness of bread, and abundance of idleness was in her and in her daughters, neither did she strengthen the hand of the poor and needy. And they were haughty, and committed abomination before me: therefore I took them away as I saw good. Neither hath Samaria committed half of thy sins; but thou hast multiplied thine abominations more than they, and hast justified thy sisters in all thine abominations which thou hast done. (Ezekiel 16:49–51)

The Pharisees also came unto him, tempting him, and saying unto him, Is it lawful for a man to put away his wife for every cause? And he answered and said unto them, Have ye not read, that he which made them at the beginning made them male and female, And said, For this cause shall a man leave father and mother, and shall cleave to his wife: and they twain shall be one flesh? Wherefore they are no more twain, but one flesh.

What therefore God hath joined together, let not man put asunder.

They say unto him, Why did Moses then command to give a writing of divorcement, and to put her away? He saith unto them, Moses because of the hardness of your hearts suffered you to put away your wives: but from the beginning it was not so. (Matthew 19:3–8)

For the wrath of God is revealed from heaven against all ungodliness and unrighteousness of men, who hold the truth in unrighteousness; Because that which may be known of God is manifest in them; for God hath shewed it unto them.

Wherefore God also gave them up to uncleanness through the lusts of their own hearts, to dishonour their own bodies between themselves: Who changed the truth of God into a lie, and worshipped and served the creature more than the Creator, who is blessed for ever. Amen. For this cause God gave them up unto vile affections: for even their women did change the natural use into that which is against nature: And likewise also the men, leaving the natural use of the woman, burned in their lust one toward another; men with men working that which is unseemly, and receiving in themselves that recompence of their error which was meet.

And even as they did not like to retain God in their knowledge, God gave them over to a reprobate mind, to do those things which are not convenient;
Being filled with all unrighteousness, fornication, wickedness, covetousness, maliciousness; full of envy, murder, debate, deceit, malignity; whisperers, Backbiters,

haters of God, despiteful, proud, boasters, inventors of evil things, disobedient to parents, Without understanding, covenantbreakers, without natural affection, implacable, unmerciful: Who knowing the judgment of God, that they which commit such things are worthy of death, not only do the same, but have pleasure in them that do them. (Romans 1:24–32)

Know ye not that the unrighteous shall not inherit the kingdom of God? Be not deceived: neither fornicators, nor idolaters, nor adulterers, nor effeminate, nor abusers of themselves with mankind, Nor thieves, nor covetous, nor drunkards, nor revilers, nor extortioners, shall inherit the kingdom of God. And such were some of you: but ye are washed, but ye are sanctified, but ye are justified in the name of the Lord Jesus, and by the Spirit of our God. (1 Corinthians 6:9–11)

Now the works of the flesh are manifest, which are these; Adultery, fornication, uncleanness, lasciviousness. (Galatians 5:19)

But fornication, and all uncleanness, or covetousness, let it not be once named among you, as becometh saints; Neither filthiness, nor foolish talking, nor jesting, which are not convenient: but rather giving of thanks. For this ye know, that no whoremonger, nor unclean person, nor covetous man, who is an idolater, hath any inheritance in the kingdom of Christ and of God. Let no man deceive you with vain words: for because of these things cometh the wrath of God upon the children of disobedience. Be not ye therefore partakers with them. (Ephesians 5:3–7) Mortify therefore your members which are upon the earth; fornication, uncleanness, inordinate affection, evil concupiscence, and covetousness, which is idolatry: For which things' sake the wrath of God cometh on the children of disobedience: In the which ye also walked some time, when ye lived in them. (Colossians 3:5—7)

But we know that the law is good, if a man use it lawfully; Knowing this, that the law is not made for a righteous man, but for the lawless and disobedient, for the ungodly and for sinners, for unholy and profane, for murderers of fathers and murderers of mothers, for manslayers, For whoremongers, for them that defile themselves with mankind, for menstealers, for liars, for perjured persons, and if there be any other thing that is contrary to sound doctrine. (1 Timothy 1:8—10)

Now the Spirit speaketh expressly, that in the latter times some shall depart from the faith, giving heed to seducing spirits, and doctrines of devils; Speaking lies in hypocrisy; having their conscience seared with a hot iron; Forbidding to marry, and commanding to abstain from meats, which God hath created to be received with thanksgiving of them which believe and know the truth. (1 Timothy 4:1—3)

Unto the pure all things are pure: but unto them that are defiled and unbelieving is nothing pure; but even their mind and conscience is defiled. They profess that they know God; but in works they deny him, being abominable, and disobedient, and unto every good work reprobate. (Titus 1:15—16)
For there are certain men crept in unawares, who were before of old ordained to this condemnation, ungodly men, turning the grace of our God into lasciviousness, and denying the only Lord God, and our Lord Jesus

Christ. … Even as Sodom and Gomorrha, and the cities about them in like manner, giving themselves over to fornication, and going after strange flesh, are set forth for an example, suffering the vengeance of eternal fire. (Jude 1:4, 7)

How that they told you there should be mockers in the last time, who should walk after their own ungodly lusts. These be they who separate themselves, sensual, having not the Spirit. (Jude 1:18–19)

And there shall in no wise enter into it any thing that defileth, neither whatsoever worketh abomination, or maketh a lie: but they which are written in the Lamb's book of life. (Revelation 21:27)

Unfortunately, however, on June 26, 2015, the government of the United States of America, via the ruling of the Supreme Court, formally legalized gay marriage in the USA. Since then some western European nations have followed suit. As a result, it is beginning to be common to see two men or two women living together as a married couple. But because it is impossible for gay male couples to have children in the absence of a woman, they adopt children from various sources.

On the contrary, a lesbian couple may decide that one of them will bear a child for them by engaging the services of, or playing games with, a man who is not allowed to return later to claim the child; on the other hand they may acquire sperm from a donor or a sperm bank and do in vitro fertilization in order to have children, but avoid living with a man. This involves artificial insemination, which Wikipedia describes as the "deliberate introduction of sperm [obtained from a donor or a sperm bank] into a female's uterus or cervix for the purpose of achieving a pregnancy through in vivo fertilization by means other than sexual intercourse."[8] Lesbian couples also may adopt children instead of one of them carrying a baby in her womb.

4.4 Single-Parent Family

A single-parent family is a family phenomenon in which a child or children live(s) together with only one parent at a time. Single- parent families have become more common and popular in the United States in particular and in the advanced/Western countries of the world in general. In times past people were introduced as "my wife" or "my husband." But in recent times you often hear things like, "Meet the mom of my kids," "This is the father of my child[ren]," or "Here is my boyfriend [or girlfriend]."

These kinds of introductions result from the fact that many man–woman (sexual) relationships that result in pregnancies do not end up in marriage. Oftentimes, when they do, as is the case with most of them, they end in separation or divorce, and it has to be determined, mostly by a court of law, which of the parents should have custody of the child(ren). And most of the time it is the mother who is awarded custody. Generally, the court mandates the parent who loses custody to regularly pay a certain percentage of his or her income for child support or alimony to the other parent for a certain number of years, usually until the (youngest) child turns twenty-one years of age. So, only the parent who has custody brings up the child(ren).

There are other causes of single-parent families to be looked into later.

---

[8] "Artificial Insemination," Wikipedia, last updated February 1, 2018, https://en.wikipedia.org/wiki/Artificial_insemination.

4.5 Cohabitation

Cohabit has its root in the Latin *habito-are*, which means "to coexist or to dwell together." So, cohabitation is a situation in which people live together for romantic or sexual reasons. Generally cohabitation involves two people of the opposite sex (before gay relationships became openly acceptable in some quarters) who, not being married, live together as if married and do most or all of the things married couples do.

Some cohabit and eventually get married, while others cohabit perpetually until they are separated by death or other factors that often lead married couples to divorce. Cohabiters never address each other as "husband" or "wife," but as "my boyfriend" or "my girlfriend," "my partner," or "the father [or mother] of my child," as the case may be. They may have children, for whose sake some of such cohabiters consider formalizing marriage or else get separated.

The major "advantages" of cohabitation are as follows:

- **Freedom.** As there is no legally binding commitment between the couple, each of them appears to be free to do things not allowed in formal marriage or not characteristic of formally married couples.
- **Study time.** Some claim that while living together, they study each other to ascertain their compatibility before proceeding into marriage.
- **cost.** The relationship is cheap to enter into in that the couple doesn't go through the demands of engagement and a marriage ceremony.
- **no alimony.** If the cohabiters break up, as they are more likely to do, neither of them is likely required to pay alimony, all things being equal.

Although, as usual, society gives cohabitation its approval or overlooks it, it remains true that any sexual relationship outside of marriage is sinful before God. It is fornication or adultery (as the case may be). Such persons perpetually live in sin. It is dangerous to enjoy the seeming benefits of cohabitation at the cost of one's soul. Jesus Christ asked, "For what shall it profit a man, if he shall gain the whole world [enjoy this life], and lose his own soul?" (Mark 8:36). The Bible says, "The soul that sinneth, it shall die. The son shall not bear the iniquity of the father, neither shall the father bear the iniquity of the son: the righteousness of the righteous shall be upon him, and the wickedness of the wicked shall be upon him" (Ezekiel 18:20).

4.6 Two-Parent Family With Blurred Parental Roles

Normally all the constituent members of the family have natural roles. Traditionally the father is breadwinner for the family. He goes to work to earn money for the running of the family. The apostle Paul says that if any man[9] fails to provide for his people, especially for members of his own household, he has denied the faith and is worse than an unbeliever (1 Timothy 5:8). At the same time, the traditional role of the mother is to care for the home, including raising the children and tending to the household chores.

However, with the rise of, and increase in the pursuance of, careers by women in workplaces outside the home, household chores

---

[9] The King James Version translates the Greek word τις (*tis*) as "any," which, according to some, can mean "anybody"—man or woman, boy or girl. The Weymouth New Testament translates the word as "a man," and the Douay–Rheims Bible says it is "any man." Most of the other "modern" Bible versions or translations say it is "anyone," "someone," "anybody," or some other term that could imply man or woman in line with the feminist demands on Bible translation.

It is assumed in 1 Timothy 5:8 that the KJV's *any* implies *any man* in view of the antecedents going back to chapter 3. The same Greek word, *tis*, is translated "any man" in 1 Timothy 3:5 (KJV). Additionally, all three pronouns after *any* in 1 Timothy 5:8 are masculine—*his*, *him*, and *he*.

in many families are now shared with, or switched to, the fathers. Furthermore, there are instances of the wife playing the role of breadwinner with the husband as a stay-at-home dad. In this case there is a total switch in roles: he cares for the home and children.

Where both parents are employed, depending on their work schedules, their roles in the home become somehow blurred. Financing of the bills is shared. Household chores may be shared. Child upbringing and care, such as doing school runs, may be alternated or totally switched.

These days, with the rise in the numbers of single mothers, the roles of mothers and grown-up children in the home have become blurred as they share family roles and responsibilities.

A great deal of these family models are designed by the devil as an attack on God's work and on the ideal family, where the man and his wife have children whom the man and his wife should raise in the fear and nurture of the Lord.

CHAPTER 5

REASONS FOR AVOIDANCE OF MARRIAGE

IN ORDER TO CARRY OUT THE WILL AND ORDER OF God—to be fruitful, multiply, and replenish the earth (Genesis 1:28)—marriage is a requirement. But many young people these days avoid getting married. Of course this is not surprising, because the apostle Paul said, in fact predicted, as follows: "Now the Spirit speaketh expressly, that in the latter times some shall depart from the faith, giving heed to seducing spirits, and doctrines of devils; Speaking lies in hypocrisy; having their conscience seared with a hot iron; Forbidding to marry, and commanding to abstain from meats, which God hath created to be received with thanksgiving of them which believe and know the truth" (1 Timothy 4:1–3).

> *He also said, "This know also, that in the last days perilous times shall come. For men shall be lovers of their own selves, covetous, boasters, proud, blasphemers, disobedient to parents, unthankful, unholy, Without natural affection, trucebreakers, false accusers, incontinent, fierce, despisers of those that are good, Traitors, heady, highminded, lovers of pleasures more than lovers of God; Having a form of godliness, but denying the power thereof: from such turn away." (2 Timothy 3:1–5)*

Apart from reasons of false teaching received by unmarried persons, some excuses for avoiding marriage are discussed in the following sections.

5.1 Fear of the Unknown

Thinking about marriage, there are a lot of unknowns concerning the future. Fear of the unknown generally is termed in psychology as xenophobia. It is difficult to predict accurately what the future holds for any marriage. Following are questions that people considering marriage may ask themselves: -

a) What is the guarantee that my husband will not become a wife beater or a drunkard (alcoholic)?

b) Is there any assurance that this "for-better-for-worse" commitment will be blessed with children? And if not, what shall I do?

c) Will my spouse remain faithful? What is the assurance that my spouse will not continue to have sexual relations with his [or her] former girlfriends [boyfriends]? What will I do if I should discover that my spouse cheating; how could I stand it?

d) Suppose we get married hoping that we will become richer than we are as single persons, but what if this doesn't happen?

How will we cope? What if the economy grows worse? How will I cope if I have a family?

e)   How can I be sure we will have good children who will not become rebellious and burdensome?

f)   What will be the attitude of my parents-in-law and my siblings-in-law toward me? Will they be welcoming, loving, and caring or antagonizing? Will they be too demanding and overbearing?

For these and many other fears, some young people avoid being committed in marriage to someone else. As long as these fears are not overcome, marriage is not possible.

There is one solution to xenophobia: even if we don't know what tomorrow will bring, we do know and trust in the One (God) who holds tomorrow. The apostle Paul says, "I can do all things through Christ which strengtheneth me" (Philippians 4:13).

5.2 Poor World Economy

Some people of marriageable age avoid marriage because they fear a poor economy, which affects individuals. As many economies keep on dwindling, unemployment grows. Many young people secure long-term unemployment after graduation from whatever institution of learning. Such young persons do not want to add to their burden by marrying. One may ask why he should marry, only to bring into this world of too many uncertainties children, for whom he is unsure he has the resources to raise. In fact, many such young people remain dependent on their parents for a long time. And many parents are willing to finance a married adult son or daughter.

On the other hand, many who work earn too little money to enable them to meet their regular general expenses. But a young man who doesn't have wealthy parents wants to be sure that he can fend for himself before taking a wife. A young woman wants to be sure that the young man who intends to marry her has the means to take care of her, or that she has a firm standing, before she will agree to enter into marriage with him. Unfortunately, by the time the situation improves, these people have become too old or are too used to singleness to reconsider marriage. So they remain permanently unmarried.

5.3 Fear of Loss of Personal Freedom

Some people love freedom so much that they do not want to be committed to a relationship that could interfere with such freedom. They may want to be free to relate with, and date, as many people as possible for as long as they want. Such persons may want to be free to do what they like with their finances, time, and bodies. This desire for absolute freedom results in an unwillingness to be committed to a spouse, as people of this sort do not want to be controlled by someone else.

Equally, some such freedom-loving persons do not want to be bothered by children and their demands, and hence they are not interested in bearing children. But the funny thing about them is that they don't mind keeping and caring for domestic animals as pets for various purposes.

5.4 Impotence And Infertility (Including Eunuchs)

You may meet a man, a bit advanced in age, who has refused to be married and does not reveal his reason. He might continue to say he would marry at the right time, but he never does. Such a man does not associate closely with any women so as he is not expected to be aroused. An investigation would reveal that such a man is impotent and does not want to put the future of any woman in jeopardy, or let out his personal secret, so he remains unmarried.

Similarly, a woman who has lost her uterus for any reason, such as sexual promiscuity that results in too many abortions, may not want to expose herself by getting married to a man who may expect pregnancy after some time in the marriage. If there is no marriage, she has no reason to tell any partner of her past.

These days, as trial marriage has become popular, a young couple courting for a long time may not want to formalize marriage until and unless the woman is pregnant. This is to ensure that the woman is fertile, with the couple probably not believing that either of them could be infertile. They may wait for years on end, remaining boyfriend and girlfriend ad infinitum.

5.5 Celibacy

Celibacy is defined as the state of voluntarily remaining unmarried and abstaining from sexual relations, especially on religious grounds. This practice is more pronounced in Roman Catholicism, where young men who become priests and young women who become nuns vow to remain unmarried in their service to God. This normally involves abstention from sexual intercourse. Whether every one of them remains faithful to this vow is a different matter. The Bible says that celibacy is a gift of God, thus: "For I would that all men were even as I myself. But every man hath his proper gift of God, one after this manner, and another after that. I say therefore to the unmarried and widows, it is good for them if they abide even as I. But if they cannot contain, let them marry: for it is better to marry than to burn. But as God hath distributed to every man, as the Lord hath called every one, so let him walk. And so ordain I in all churches" (1 Corinthians 7:7–9, 17).

Further along in the same Bible chapter, the apostle Paul talks of the advantages of celibacy in contrast to marriage of women, as follows:

> *But I would have you without carefulness. He that is unmarried careth for the things that belong to the Lord, how he may please the Lord: But he that is married careth*

for the things that are of the world, how he may please his wife. There is difference also between a wife and a virgin. The unmarried woman careth for the things of the Lord, that she may be holy both in body and in spirit: but she that is married careth for the things of the world, how she may please her husband. And this I speak for your own profit; not that I may cast a snare upon you, but for that which is comely, and that ye may attend upon the Lord without distraction. (1 Corinthians 7:32–35)

Jesus Christ explained how and why celibacy arises: "His disciples say unto him, If the case of the man be so with his wife, it is not good to marry. But he said unto them, All men cannot receive this saying, save they to whom it is given. For there are some eunuchs, which were so born from their mother's womb: and there are some eunuchs, which were made eunuchs of men: and there be eunuchs, which have made themselves eunuchs for the kingdom of heaven's sake. He that is able to receive it, let him receive it" (Matthew 19:10–12).

However, celibacy could also arise from deceit, as the apostle Paul wrote to Timothy: "Now the Spirit speaketh expressly, that in the latter times some shall depart from the faith, giving heed to seducing spirits, and doctrines of devils; Speaking lies in hypocrisy; having their conscience seared with a hot iron; Forbidding to marry, and commanding to abstain from meats, which God hath created to be received with thanksgiving of them which believe and know the truth" (1 Timothy 4:1–3).

5.6 Influence Of The Women's Liberation Movement/Feminist Movement

Two names or phrases to be used in this section, sometimes interchangeably, are women's liberation movement (WLM) and feminist movement (FM). Wikipedia, in its definition, says that the feminist movement is also known as the women's liberation movement "or simply feminism."[1] Conversely, Jo Freeman, in a paper titled "The Women's Liberation Movement: Its Origin, Structures, and Ideas," which was presented "at several universities and colleges in the Midwest in 1970," writes, "In many ways there were two separate movements which only in the last year have merged sufficiently for the rubric 'women's liberation' to be truly an umbrella term for the multiplicity of organizations and groups."[2]

WLM reemerged in the United States and other developed countries in the late 1960s and early 1970s. Linda Napikoski, in her article "The Women's Liberation Movement—A History of Feminism in the 1960s and 1970s," describes the movement as one "by women purposed for collectively struggling for equality [with men] and for seeking freedom from oppression and male supremacy and domination."[3] An online dictionary defines *liberation* as "the act of setting someone free from imprisonment, slavery, or oppression." So, WLM's campaigns are aimed at setting women free from perceived slavery and oppression—discrimination, inequalities, etc. *Webster's All-in-One Dictionary and Thesaurus* defines *feminism* as "the organized activity on behalf of women's rights and interests."[4] The series of organized campaigns in various forms in different nations of the world that have concerned themselves with the rights and interests of women are termed feminism or the feminist movement. Both women and men have been involved in feminism.

---

[1] "Feminist Movement," Wikipedia, last updated February 25, 2018, https://en.wikipedia.org/wiki/Feminist_movement.

[2] Jo Freeman, "The Women's Liberation Movement: Its Origins, Structures, and Ideas," accessed April 30, 2018, http://www.jofreeman.com/feminism/liberationmov.htm.

[3] Linda Napikoski. The Women's Liberation Movement - A History of Feminism in the 1960s and 1970s
Accessed April 24, 2018, https://www.thoughtco.com/womens-liberation-movement-3528926.

[4] *Webster's All-in-One Dictionary and Thesaurus*, (2010), s.v. "feminism."

There are indications that feminism existed in some European nations in the eighteenth century. It began to gain ground in the USA in the 1950s, along with other civil rights movements. However, the WLM became more popular late in the 1960s, when women rediscovered and read *The Second Sex* by Simone de Beauvoir (published in 1949 and translated into English for the first time in 1953). That author was said to be a women's rights defender.[5] The areas of concentration of the movement include the following:

- Political and legal rights encompassing the following:
  - Female suffrage (the right to vote and be voted for). This arose because in most countries women were not allowed to vote or stand for election.
  - Civil rights—equal rights with men, including the right to inherit and to own property, as well as have financial rights; equal employment opportunities and equal pay for equal work.

- Right to education
  In the USA and Europe, until the late 1800s, except for the wealthy, women were not given access to education beyond primary (elementary) school. Although by the 1950s some women had a college education, they were still mostly bound to domestic duties.[6]

  - Social issues—such as glass ceiling[7] and sexual harassment—arose. As more women began to make

---

[5] "Feminist Movement," Wikipedia, accessed April 24, 2018, https://en.wikipedia.org/wiki/Feminist_Movement.

[6] Natasha Thomsen, *Global Issues: Women's Rights* (New York: Facts on File, 2007), 6.

[7] The glass ceiling is an unofficial but known barrier to the advancement of certain people (often women and minority groups) beyond certain career levels.

careers with paid employment, proponents of the feminist movement felt that women were discriminated against (i.e., treated as inferior to their male counterparts in spite of their education). Sexual harassment (the making of unwanted sexual advances or offensive or disgusting remarks to a woman), of which the definition and interpretation today continues to be "expanded," also became an issue to fight against in the workplace. So, women have to be protected from behaviors of men toward them that affect the women physically and emotionally. With the passing of time, sexual harassment regulations are being abused (more so in the twenty-first century), even in the political arena. Women also wanted to join and be involved in the military like their male counterparts. A popular saying credited to the WLM is, "What a man can do, a woman also can do, and even better."

- Family health and sexuality
Feminism insists that everyone owns his or her own body, implying that a woman has the right to choose what to do with her body, rather than be controlled by some man. This right to choose should extend to the woman's reproductive rights, the right to decide whether to bear children or not, the number of children a woman will have, and whether or not to carry to term or terminate a pregnancy. By extension the woman has the right to be married or stay unmarried, use contraceptives, and/or patronize abortion clinics if needed.

The Wikipedia article "Feminist Movement in Western Society" talks of an article published in *Birth Control Review* in 1918 by Crystal Eastman in which she "contended that birth control is a fundamental right for women and must be available as an alternative if they are to participate in the modern world."[8]

Natasha Thomsen, in *Global Issues: Women's Rights*, observes that gender roles in the family have been redefined in developed countries since the 1970s because of higher education [of women] and employment opportunities, which have resulted in delayed marriage, smaller households, delay in childbearing, a decline in birth rates, and an increase in divorce and single parenthood.[9]

- Other social and cultural issues
  Other issues pursued by feminist movements that could be classified as social, cultural, and religious and that were/are not applicable to some nations include, but are not limited to, the following:
  - Paid maternity leave for working mothers
  - Violence (especially domestic) against women, rape, and sexual abuse, either by spouses or others
  - Human (especially women) trafficking and prostitution
  - Female circumcision (a.k.a. female genital mutilation), a practice by which a girl's whole clitoris or its hood is cut off. In some cultures this stems from the belief that a woman becomes uncontrollably promiscuous if uncircumcised (because of the assumption that with the clitoris within easy reach and touch, she can be easily turned on).
  - Leadership roles in religious organizations that did not allow women such opportunities

---

[8] "Feminist Movement," Wikipedia, accessed May 1, 2018, https://en.wikipedia.org/wiki/Feminist_movement.
[9] Thomsen, *Global Issues: Women's Rights*, 16.

Feminist/women's liberation movements have over the years achieved a lot in terms of the issues listed above and other issues. Of course, these achievements have fueled or led to the successes of other movements and abuses within society, but time and space limit their inclusion in this work. Some of the achievements and effects of the feminist movement will be highlighted next.

Successes of the Feminist Movement

The feminist movement has been totally or partially successful in most of its endeavors and campaigns in various parts of the world. Many of the achievements have affected society, its shape, and its modes of life immensely. While some of the results are positive, others are negative. Without much elaboration, some of the successes are as follows:

- Women's suffrage in most Western nations. In the USA in 2016, a woman, Hillary Rodham Clinton, made history. "In July 2016, she became the first woman to earn a major party's nomination for president, and went on to earn 66 million votes"[10] (about 3 million more votes than her opponent). She was the Democratic Party's final candidate for the presidential election in which Donald J. Trump was declared winner by the electoral college and was inaugurated the forty-sixth president of the United States on January 20, 2017. Most women were registered to vote, and many others sought elected posts. Interestingly, for the 2020 presidential election, twenty-four Democrats were registered for nomination, out of which five were women.
- The right to education to any level in all Western countries. Many other countries, or areas of them, are still struggling with this.

---

[10] The Office of Hillary Rodham Clinton: About Hillary. Accessed January 21, 2019 https://www.hillaryclinton.com/about/.

– Equal employment/career opportunities with equal pay for equal work, and the war against sexual harassment.

– The right to own property and personal finances.

– Maternity leave for working mothers. Some employers are still struggling with allowing this with pay since most wages are based on hours worked during a pay period.

– Freedom of marriage and the right to birth control, contraceptives, and/or an abortion.

– The right to initiate divorce; also the right to a no-fault divorce—a kind of divorce case whereby the filing spouse is not obligated to prove any fault on the part of the other spouse.

– Freedom of women to bear children out of wedlock—an outcome of reproductive rights—and freedom to choose what to do with one's body.

– Outlawing female genital mutilation (female circumcision).

– Imposition/adoption of gender-inclusive and gender-neutral terms like *humanity* in place of *mankind*, and third-person plural pronouns (*they* and *them*) in place of *he* and *him* where the gender of the subject is not known. A nonsexist title for women—Ms.—is now used for all females, whether single or married, robbing married women of the respect that was accorded them when "Mrs." Prefixed their names. It is noteworthy that these gender-neutral or gender-exclusive terms have been applied in some recent translations of the Bible in comparison to the Authorized King James Version of 1611. For example, compare the following two translations:

• "But as many as received him, to them gave he power to become *the sons of God*, even to them that believe on his name" (John 1:12 KJV; emphasis added).

• "Yet to all who did receive him, to those who believed in his name, he gave the right to become *children of God* " (John 1:12 NIV; emphasis added).

Samuel Gipp, ThD, observed, while comparing the Authorized King James Version of 1611 and the New King James Version, that in the First Epistle to the Corinthians alone—one of twenty-seven books of the New Testament—gender has been excluded as many as forty two times. Some of such occurrences are listed as follows:[11]

authorized King James Version	new King James Version
Many wise men (1 Cor. 1:26)	Many wise
Man's wisdom (1 Cor. 2:4)	Human wisdom
No man (1 Cor. 2:15)	No one
Every man (1 Cor. 3:5)	Each one
No man (1 Cor. 3:11)	Anyone
Man's judgment (1 Cor. 4:3)	Human court
Think of men beyond (1 Cor. 4:6)	Think beyond ("men" was deleted)
Some man (1 Cor. 15:35)	Someone
Any man (1 Cor. 16:22)	Anyone

- Involvement in traditional church and other religious practices and occupying some offices previously held only by men, such as ordained female priests or pastors/bishops in some denominations.
- Equality of men and women (husband and wife). One is not superior to the other. This leads to sharing of household chores and family responsibilities, which are no longer defined along sex lines.
- Sexual relationships should be at the whims and caprices of the woman, otherwise it could be interpreted as rape, sexual harassment, and/or improper or indecent touching or speech.

---

[11] Samuel C. Gipp, *Gipp's Understandable History of the Bible* (Miamitown, OH: DayStar, 2004), 389–90.

With the success of feminism in these and other unlisted areas of its campaigns, a great deal of change has occurred and has been occurring in the family structure. Many times, too much exercise of these rights and freedoms of women tends to insult and frustrate some husbands, who see such actions as an infringement on their naturally endowed authority as men. This sort of situation usually ends in separation or divorce.

The FM/WLM has so influenced the justice system in most Western nations that the courts appear to be generally very sympathetic with women, to the extent that at the slightest provocation, a divorce suit can be initiated and is almost certain to end in favor of the woman. Divorce suits and alimony have impoverished many men. Most of such divorce suits may leave custody of the children to one of the spouses, thereby creating another single-parent family.

Women are no longer stigmatized for, or ashamed of, pregnancy outside marriage, giving rise to an increase in the number of unmarried mothers who singlehandedly parent their children.

The fear of a possible divorce suit that could result in loss of peace of mind and property, bring frustration and loneliness, cause a person to have to begin again, and lead to an inability to trust another now makes men view committing themselves in marriage with trepidation. This culminates in many unmarried fathers and mothers as parents. The couple may continue their relationship as boyfriend and girlfriend, leading them to sometimes introduce each other as "father of my child" or "mother of my child" rather than "my husband" or "my wife."

Feminist-Motivated Excuses Not to Marry

Feminism has, to a great extent, influenced many women to decide not to marry. This has been done by means of propagating such messages as to create fear and discouragement in young women. In addition, many young women are taking their cue from their parents' poisoned minds. By the way, the Bible says, "Now the Spirit speaketh expressly, that in the latter times some shall depart from the faith, giving heed to seducing spirits, and doctrines of devils; Speaking lies in hypocrisy; having their conscience seared with a hot iron; Forbidding to marry" (1 Timothy 4:1–3).

In the article "11 Reasons to *Not* Get Married," Susan Cox[12] proffers some reasons for avoiding marriage, including the following:

(1) Marriage still subordinates a woman to the man: she changes her home to his, and she changes her last name (unless she insists on keeping her maiden name, thanks to the feminist movement); she also changes her relationships and lifestyle. The likely change in the man's lifestyle, on the other hand, is next to nothing. When a woman gets married, she loses all her freedom in life!

(2) When a woman gets married, the children of the marriage are owned by the man, whose name they bear, and the woman loses out.

(3) Marriage is still the same old legal and social patriarchal institution where the man has all the benefits and remains in control of the woman as a piece of property.

(4) When a man gets married, his employer considers him a more mature, responsible man, stable and fit for higher responsibilities. On the contrary, the employer looks at the newly married woman with suspicion, considering that she might soon bear children and begin to place her children and family ahead of her work. That would affect her progress in her career while her husband is moving up.

(5) A married woman is not better than an unmarried woman. After all, the married woman is encumbered with caring for her husband, an adult, like a child just as if she were his

---

[12] Susan Cox. Feminist Current: *"11 Reasons to NOT get married"*
Accessed April 24, 2018, http://www.feministcurrent.com/2016/02/12/11-reasons-not-to-get-married/.

mother. This is in view of the fact that most husbands can hardly do many things for, and by, themselves.

(6) Marriage promotes, rather than eliminates or prevents, loneliness. The man is no longer as available as he used to be while in courtship with the woman. And being married, she can't go out with just anybody when her husband is not there. Even when there are children in the marriage, they do not play the husband's role of providing company. To remain a spinster does not imply solitude or a life of emptiness since one can find friendship, children, and family in the community.

(7) Marriage destroys a couple's sex life a few months after its commencement. While the woman makes efforts to meet and satisfy the sexual demands of her husband, he may not be equally forthcoming. And when he is not there, the woman cannot go elsewhere to satisfy her own sexual needs. But the unmarried woman can get all she wants sexually from a temporary relationship and end the relationship when the man is no longer forthcoming.

(8) While it is very simple and easy to get tied into marriage, it is time-consuming, heartbreaking, and full of hassles to obtain a divorce. You can more easily part ways with a boyfriend, being not legally committed, than with a husband.

(9) Men are generally unfaithful to their wives, and no woman is ever pleased seeing another woman messing around with the man to whom she (the wife) is devoted. You can easily kick out an unfaithful boyfriend and have peace.

CHAPTER 6

THE MAKING OF SINGLE PARENTS

IN HER ARTICLE, "THE SINGLE PARENT STATISTICS BASED on Census Data" Jennifer Wolf noted that the U.S. census of 2015 published in 2018 revealed that there were approximately 13.7 million single parents in the United States then, and they had about 22.4 million children (about 27 percent of all children below age 21) living with them. It's further revealed that while mothers constituted about 80.4 percent of custodial parents, only 19.6 percent were fathers.[1]

The Space-out Scientist, quoting the Organization for Economic Co-operation and Development (OECD, 2014) wrote in the article dated July 18 2018, titled "Single parents worldwide: Statistics

---

[1] Jennifer Wolf. "The Single Parent Statistics Based on Census Data," accessed November 11, 2019. https://www.verywellfamily.com/single-parent-census-data-2997668 Updated September 13, 2019.

and trends" that 17 percent of children aged 14 years and under lived in single parent households worldwide, and approximately 88 percent of such households were headed by women. This account, corroborating Wolf's, says that by 2016 27 percent of children under age 18 lived in single parent households in the US, 80 percent of which (households) were headed by women, while 4 percent of children were raised [by their fathers] without their mothers. Also the Canadian 2016 census revealed that 19.2 percent of all Canadian children lived with single parents. 81.3 percent of these children lived with their mothers and 18.7 percent lived with their fathers.[2]

Previously we discussed what single parenting is. In this chapter we will consider two broad causes of single-parent families:

- single parenting due to circumstances beyond control
- single parenting by choice

6.1 unavoidable circumstances or circumstances beyond control

Sickness, death, incarceration of one spouse, and immigration are some of the circumstances beyond control that culminate in single-parent families, to be discussed here.

6.1.1 *Death of One Parent*

When the husband or the wife dies while their children are still growing up, the bereaved partner has to singlehandedly carry on the family's affairs and projects, including child upbringing. A change in this single-parent status can only occur if the bereaved spouse remarries. Depending on the age of this living spouse, a remarriage

---

[2] *The Space-out Scientist.* "Single parents worldwide: Statistics and trends," accessed November 11, 2019. https://spacedoutscientist.com/2017/07/18/ single-parents-worldwide-statistics-and-trends/.

is actually advisable in order to prevent loneliness, which normally sets in when the children are mature and leave the home.

6.1.2 *Sickness*

Illness is another circumstance beyond control that is capable of leading to single parenting. Prolonged or terminal illness, which keeps the ill spouse away from home and in the hospital, in a nursing home, or elsewhere, subjects the healthy spouse to carrying on with the affairs of the family alone.

6.1.3 *Incarceration (Imprisonment)*

Incarceration of one of the two spouses is another uncontrollable[3] circumstance under consideration. Depending on the terms of the incarceration, the one jailed may be away for a long time—many months or many years, or even for life—so that by the time of release, the children may have all grown up and left home, having become independent adults. Unlike in the case of death, the free parent cannot legitimately remarry while the spouse is in jail. This is because the jailed spouse could be pardoned or may complete his or her jail term and return home. The family of the onetime president of South Africa is a good case in point.

Dr. Nelson Mandela was born in 1918. At the age of forty-six, in 1964, Mandela was sentenced to life imprisonment by the apartheid regime in South Africa. He was released in 1990 at age seventy-two. Certainly he had a wife and children before his incarceration. Even though that imprisonment was politically motivated, nobody was sure Mandela would come out alive. But at the time of his release, his children, whom his wife had had to singlehandedly bring up, had begun to have children, having gone out to live on their own.

---

[3] The circumstances leading to imprisonment can often be avoided. But when a parent is sentenced, his or her absence from the home becomes unavoidable or uncontrollable.

6.1.4 *War, Immigration, and Other Relocation Situations*

War does separate husband and wife such that one of them and some or all of their children stay together with one spouse alone caring for them. This situation might remain in place until the war ends. Similarly, a spouse could travel abroad to study or work while the other spouse remains at home, raising the children alone. This might appear to be for a temporary period of time, but sometimes it could become permanent or drag on till the children are mature and begin to leave home. The immigration laws of the nation in question could cause a couple to remain separated for an indefinite length of time and make one of the spouses live as a single parent with the children.

These examples of causes of single-parent families are not as impactful as when one spouse dies. In these former cases, there is the hope that one day the missing spouse may be reunited with the rest of the family.

However, the Bible advises that temporary separation of spouses should not endure for too long a time in order to prevent temptations that could arise. It reads, "Defraud ye not one the other, except it be with consent for a time, that ye may give yourselves to fasting and prayer; and come together again, that Satan tempt you not for your incontinency" (1 Corinthians 7:3–5).

For parents finding themselves single because of death of the spouse, biblical counsel is found in the following two passages:

- "Now concerning the things whereof ye wrote unto me: It is good for a man not to touch a woman. Nevertheless, to avoid fornication, let every man have his own wife, and let every woman have her own husband" (1 Corinthians 7:1–2).
- "I will therefore that the younger women marry, bear children, guide the house, give none occasion to the adversary to speak reproachfully" (1 Timothy 5:14).

6.1.5 Societal Depravity

As moral laxity in society is growing worse by the day due to what has been termed "development" or "civilization," there is also an increase in incidences that bring about unwanted pregnancies, some of which lead to unplanned children. Examples of these incidences are rape, incest, and prostitution.

An unknown or unaccepted man may rape a girl or a woman, an act that could result in pregnancy. For fear of committing murder or of the future health consequences of abortion, the girl or woman may not want to terminate the pregnancy. After the baby is born, the mother may never find a man to marry or may become too afraid to live with a man. She then has to bring up her child singlehandedly. Incest is another moral ill that is capable of causing single parenthood, just like rape. However, incest differs from rape in that the sexual act is committed by a close relative such as a father, brother, or uncle instead of by an unknown man. On the other hand, a woman who engages in prostitution or harlotry may have an accidental pregnancy arising from failure to use, or ineffectiveness of used, contraceptives. She is likely to end up bringing up the child she bears alone.

6.2 choice

As opposed to becoming a single parent because of unavoidable circumstances, there are single parents who choose to be so because of their lifestyles, or who are aware of the possible outcome of their actions but still go ahead and take such actions.

6.2.1 Sexual Immorality, Promiscuity, and Unwanted Pregnancy

A sexually promiscuous person is likely to end up with an accidental pregnancy that is undesired and unprepared for. The same applies to persons who indulge in casual sexual intercourse outside marriage. When either party to the sex act lacks interest in marriage in spite of the pregnancy that has resulted, the pregnant woman may decide to carry the pregnancy to term, bear the baby, and bring up the child alone.[4]

Until recently in most parts of Nigeria in particular, and in the world in general, pregnancy outside wedlock was taboo and was reason enough for a woman never to be approached for marriage after the baby had been delivered. In that case the woman would be a single parent.

However, on the contrary, in the Western world it has become almost impossible to find a woman to marry who does not already have a child, especially because it is considered in the United States, for example, to be—to put mildly—impolite (if not sexual harassment) to ask a woman whether she is married or has children. This has given rise to many stepchildren and stepparents, step-this and step-that. Stepparenting has its complexities and problems and carries with it more disadvantages than advantages.

Biblically, sexual immorality is a sin before God, notwithstanding the present-day positive or nonchalant attitude of society toward it. Some accidental pregnancies lead to marriage though. Yet many of such marriages often hit the rocks for various obvious reasons.

6.2.2 *Separation and Divorce*

In times past, apart from bereavement, separation and divorce were the primary factors leading to single parenting. In this context, when one of the parties of a marriage that has children separates himself or herself permanently from the spouse, the one who keeps the child(ren) brings the child(ren) up alone.

---

[4] A pregnant woman has the option these days, now that abortion has been legalized, to kill (abort) the unborn baby. But there is a limit to the number of abortions a woman can procure before she is medically advised to stop or else suffer negative health consequences.

This separation situation is akin to divorce, in which case an authority like the court permanently dissolves the marriage and assigns custody of the child(ren) to one of the erstwhile couple. Whether one of the divorcing spouses is compelled to pay for child support or not, the spouse who is given the custody becomes a single parent of the child(ren).

It should be noted, though, that the rate of divorce has been on the rise for years, especially with the "successes" thus far won by feminism/the women's liberation movement.

6.2.3 *Impatience*

Impatience is the opposite of patience, which is the act or habit of being patient. *Webster's Dictionary* defines *patient* as "bearing pain without complaining; showing self-control; or steadfast despite opposition, difficulty, or adversity."[5] Some synonyms of *patient* include being constant, steadfast, and enduring, as well as long-suffering. Impatience, therefore, implies the failure to bear pain without complaining, and the failure to show self-control or be steadfast in the face of opposition, difficulty, or adversity.

This situation applies more to women than to men. At a certain age a woman begins to feel that she is beginning to age and yet there is no suitable man to marry. She feels she should no longer continue to wait since menopause might catch up with her. Sometimes this impatience could result from pressure from family members or peers. On the other hand, the parents of a young immature man (especially an only son) may pressure their son to hurry into marriage unprepared. Many of such marriages end in divorce and are capable of creating a single-parent family.

---

[5] *Webster's Dictionary*, (2008), s.v. "patient."

6.2.4 *Misogyny and Misandry*

One may define *misogyny* as hatred for women by a man. In effect, a man who hates women is a misogynist. It is called misandry when a woman has contempt or hatred for men. Wikipedia says that misogyny manifests[6] in such ways as social exclusion, sex discrimination, hostility, androcentricism (male-centeredness), male privilege, patriarchy, belittling of women, violence against women, and sexual objectification.[7] Similarly, misandry manifests in the same, but with the opposite gender being targeted.

The effect of misogyny and misandry on a family is that the person either becomes a homosexual (gay) or merely temporarily tolerates a person of the opposite sex just for the purpose of bearing a child, only to terminate the relationship shortly afterward. A misogynist or misandrist may choose never to be married, but if they do marry, they end up becoming or creating single parents.

---

[6] "Misogyny," Wikipedia, https://en.wikipedia.org/wiki/Misogyny. Accessed June 10, 2019.

[7] Sexual objectification is defined by one online dictionary as the practice of treating someone as a mere object of sexual desire.

CHAPTER 7

THE IDEAL FAMILY IN GOD'S VIEW

THE FAMILY WAS THE FIRST INSTITUTION THAT GOD established and ordained. God had a plan and purpose for the family. God also had an ideal family in mind, which consists of husband/father, wife/mother, and child(ren). Servants may also be part of the ideal family.

The Father

And thou shalt love the Lord thy God with all thine heart, and with all thy soul, and with all thy might. And these words, which I command thee this day, shall be in thine heart: And thou shalt teach them diligently unto thy children, and shalt talk of them when thou sittest in thine house, and when thou walkest by the way, and when thou liest down, and when thou risest up. (Deuteronomy 6:5–7)

This command to Israelite fathers is a one of the many statutes that God gave the Israelites for living in the Promised Land, which they were moving into to possess. Fathers were (and are) expected to teach their children at home and, in fact, everywhere. It is required of every child to know and keep the commands of God and to live by them, not turning from them to the left or to the right, and thereby having great successes. The Bible says that God told Joshua, "This book of the law shall not depart out of thy mouth; but thou shalt meditate therein day and night, that thou mayest observe to do according to all that is written therein: for then thou shalt make thy way prosperous, and then thou shalt have good success" (Joshua 1:8).

To buttress this responsibility, the writer of Proverbs, in 22:6, admonishes, "Train up a child in the way he should go: and when he is old, he will not depart from it." The benefits that accrue therefrom as listed in the preceding five verses include a good name, loving favor, prudence, humility, and the fear of the Lord, all of which bring riches, honor, and life. The verses are as follows:

> *A good name is rather to be chosen than great riches, and loving favour rather than silver and gold. The rich and poor meet together: the Lord is the maker of them all. A prudent man foreseeth the evil, and hideth himself: but the simple pass on, and are punished. By humility and the fear of the Lord are riches, and honour, and life. Thorns and snares are in the way of the froward: he that doth keep his soul shall be far from them. (Proverbs 22:1–5)*

Some critics may argue that the instruction was to the people of Israel only. But recall that in the New Testament, Matthew recorded that when a lawyer asked Jesus Christ what the greatest commandment was, Jesus quoted the aforementioned passage from Deuteronomy 6 and added that it was the summary of the law and of the prophets (i.e., the scriptures). Here is the passage:

Then one of them, which was a lawyer, asked him a question, tempting him, and saying, Master, which is the great commandment in the law? Jesus said unto him, Thou shalt love the Lord thy God with all thy heart, and with all thy soul, and with all thy mind. This is the first and great commandment. And the second is like unto it, Thou shalt love thy neighbour as thyself. On these two commandments hang all the law and the prophets. (Matthew 22:35–40)

And the Lord said, Shall I hide from Abraham that thing which I do; Seeing that Abraham shall surely become a great and mighty nation, and all the nations of the earth shall be blessed in him? For I know him, that he will command his children and his household after him, and they shall keep the way of the Lord, to do justice and judgment; that the Lord may bring upon Abraham that which he hath spoken of him. (Genesis 18:17–19)

One of the reasons God blessed Abraham with many children is that God said that He knew that Abraham would perform proper child upbringing. The father thus has the responsibility of ensuring that all the children are properly trained:

- Sons in the home should learn from their dad to be fathers (when their time comes).
- Sons must learn from their fathers how to relate to, and care for, their wives when they become husbands.
- Sons should learn how to take and assert authority at home and wherever they find themselves.
- Sons are also taught how to provide for and manage the household in the fear of the Lord.
- Daughters learn what to expect from their future husbands from how their fathers relate with their wives (the daughters' mothers).

In the final analysis, a father must be a role model to the children (sons and daughters alike) in the home. But it becomes a different ball game when there is no father in the home. In addition to the responsibility of child training, the father is also the husband of his wife, which is a separate, enormous task, to be discussed later.

The mother

At inception God saw that it is not good for a man to be alone according to the Word of God. So, God made a helpmeet for him. Genesis 2:18 reads, "And the Lord God said, It is not good that the man should be alone; I will make him an help meet for him."

Webster's Dictionary defines *helpmeet*[1] as "the female partner in a marriage: wife."[2] However, scholars/Bible translators have variously translated the Hebrew אֵזֶר כְּנֶגְדּוֹ לוֹ —*ezer*— [for] him a helper." Examples of the translation of Genesis 2:18 are as follows (see Bible Hub's comments on the verse):[3]

- "The LORD God said, 'It is not good for the man to be alone. I will make a helper suitable for him'" (NIV).
- "Then the LORD God said, 'It is not good for the man to be alone. I will make a helper who is just right for him'" (NLT).
- "Then the LORD God said, 'It is not good that the man should be alone; I will make him a helper fit for him'" (ESV).

---

[1] Although some have suggested that the true translation of the Hebrew word transliterated *ezer* ("helper/companion") is "savior" or "deliverer," in relation to Adam, this is contestable. This is in view of the following factors: the mode of formation of Eve; the part Eve played in the temptation and fall of humankind; and the extent that the woman was going to carry in her womb the one Man who would redeem mankind.

[2] *Webster's All-in-One Dictionary and Thesaurus,* (2010), s.v. "helpmeet."

[3] Accessed June 11, 2018, http://biblehub.com/commentaries/genesis/ 2-18.htm.

- "Then the LORD God said, 'It is not good for man to be alone. I will make a helper that is right for him'" (NLV).
- "The LORD God said, 'It is not good for the man to be alone. I will make for him a suitable helper'" (BSB).
- "Then the LORD God said, 'It is not good for the man to be alone. I will make a helper corresponding to him'" (CSB).
- "The LORD God said, 'It isn't good for the man to live alone. I need to make a suitable partner for him'" (CEV).
- "Then the LORD God said, 'It is not good for the man to live alone. I will make a suitable companion to help him'" (GNT).
- "Then the LORD God said, 'It is not good for the man to be alone. I will make a helper as his complement'" (HCSB).
- "Later, the LORD God said, 'It is not good for the man to be alone. I will make the woman to be an authority corresponding to him'" (ISV).
- "Later, the LORD God said, 'It is not good for the man to be alone. I will make the woman to be an authority corresponding to him'" (NETB).
- "And the LORD God said: 'It is not good for man to be alone: let us make him a help like unto himself'" (DRAB).
- "And Jehovah God saith, 'Not good for the man to be alone, I do make to him an helper—as his counterpart'" (YLT).

In the Genesis account of creation, there does not appear to be any explicit responsibility assigned to the woman by God. Similarly, when Moses, on God's behalf, gave fathers the assignment of training their children as stated in Deuteronomy 6:5–7 (quoted above), nothing was specifically assigned to mothers. The exception is that the curse of God assigned conception with pain and sorrow to the woman. It says that God said to the woman that He would greatly multiply her sorrow and conception; and that in sorrow she would bring forth children; and her desire shall be to her husband, who shall rule over her. (Genesis 3:16).

On the other hand, a beautiful picture is painted of the ideal woman in Proverbs, as follows:

Who can find a virtuous woman? for her price is far above rubies. The heart of her husband doth safely trust in her, so that he shall have no need of spoil. She will do him good and not evil all the days of her life. She seeketh wool, and flax, and worketh willingly with her hands.

She is like the merchants' ships; she bringeth her food from afar. She riseth also while it is yet night, and giveth meat to her household, and a portion to her maidens. She considereth a field, and buyeth it: with the fruit of her hands she planteth a vineyard. She girdeth her loins with strength, and strengtheneth her arms. She perceiveth that her merchandise is good: her candle goeth not out by night. She layeth her hands to the spindle, and her hands hold the distaff. She stretcheth out her hand to the poor; yea, she reacheth forth her hands to the needy.
She is not afraid of the snow for her household: for all her household are clothed with scarlet. She maketh herself coverings of tapestry; her clothing is silk and purple. Her husband is known in the gates, when he sitteth among the elders of the land. She maketh fine linen, and selleth it; and delivereth girdles unto the merchant. Strength and honour are her clothing; and she shall rejoice in time to come. She openeth her mouth with wisdom; and in her tongue is the law of kindness.

She looketh well to the ways of her household, and eateth not the bread of idleness. Her children arise up, and call her blessed; her husband also, and he praiseth her. Many daughters have done virtuously, but thou excellest them all. Favour is deceitful, and beauty is vain: but a woman

that feareth the Lord, she shall be praised. Give her of
the fruit of her hands; and let her own works praise her
in the gates. (Proverbs 31:10–31)

All the factors that make a woman this virtuous are laudable and do contribute to the well-being of the family. Yet no woman is deemed a failure for not exhibiting all or any of the characteristics that make the woman described in Proverbs 31 virtuous; a close look at the various translations of Genesis 2:18, above, reveals that the woman is a helper of her man. Even though the various Bible translators used different terms for the type of helper God wanted to make for the man, all translators call the woman "helper" or "helpmeet."

Nevertheless, it is an ideal thing for a virtuous woman/wife to replicate herself in her daughters. It is equally important and laudable for the sons of the virtuous mother to learn her ways too, as the time will come when the sons will leave their parents to live alone, caring for themselves and their homes until married.

In the New Testament, however, the Bible encourages "that the younger women marry, bear children, guide the house, give none occasion to the adversary to speak reproachfully" (1 Timothy 5:14). This appears to be the only place in scripture where a mother is given the responsibility for the home, namely to guide the house, which could be expanded to include caretaking in general.

Technically, the upbringing of the children and caring for the family are responsibilities for the father with the assistance of his wife in the home. This conclusion assumes an ideal marriage situation in which the two parents (husband and wife) are present and live together. But occasionally the departure of one of the two dislocates this ideal situation. Unusually such a departure arises from death of one or divorce, the latter of which may be initiated by either spouse. In this case the roles of the father or the mother change.

7.1 The Ideal Family According To The Teachings of Jesus Christ

From the teachings and lifestyle of Jesus Christ, the following can be inferred as God's ideal family:

One Man, One Wife

People who have tried to bend this rule have added the phrase *at a time* to Christ's rule so as to allow themselves to have a wife and keep concubines/mistresses or to divorce and remarry, etc. They believe that as long as they live with only one officially married woman, they have complied with the rule of one man, one wife.

> *The Pharisees also came unto him [Jesus], tempting him, and saying unto him, Is it lawful for a man to put away his wife for every cause? And he answered and said unto them, Have ye not read, that he which made them at the beginning made them male and female, And said, For this cause shall a man leave father and mother, and shall cleave to his wife: and they twain shall be one flesh? Wherefore they are no more twain, but one flesh. What therefore God hath joined together, let not man put asunder. (Matthew 19:3–6)*

> *But from the beginning of the creation God made them male and female. For this cause shall a man leave his father and mother, and cleave to his wife; And they twain shall be one flesh: so then they are no more twain, but one flesh. What therefore God hath joined together, let not man put asunder. (Mark 10:6–9)*

Marriage Devoid of Adultery

Adultery is usually seen as sexual intercourse between a married person and another person (of the opposite sex). Other terms usually used to convey the adultery are *lewdness, sexual immorality, sexual impurity, sexual promiscuity,* and *fornication* (sex between unmarried individuals or sex between an unmarried person and a married person, and other forms of sexual misbehavior). However, Jesus Christ said there is more to adultery than is described here:

> *Ye have heard that it was said by them of old time, Thou shalt not commit adultery: But I say unto you, That whosoever looketh on a woman to lust after her hath committed adultery with her already in his heart. And if thy right eye offend thee, pluck it out, and cast it from thee: for it is profitable for thee that one of thy members should perish, and not that thy whole body should be cast into hell.*
>
> *And if thy right hand offend thee, cut it off, and cast it from thee: for it is profitable for thee that one of thy members should perish, and not that thy whole body should be cast into hell. It hath been said, Whosoever shall put away his wife, let him give her a writing of divorcement: But I say unto you, That whosoever shall put away his wife, saving for the cause of fornication, causeth her to commit adultery: and whosoever shall marry her that is divorced committeth adultery.* (Matthew 5:27–32)

> *He saith unto them, Moses because of the hardness of your hearts suffered you to put away your wives: but from the beginning it was not so. And I say unto you, Whosoever shall put away his wife, except it be for fornication, and shall marry another, committeth adultery: and whoso*

> *marrieth her which is put away doth commit adultery.*
> *(Matthew 19:8–9)*

However, the exception in verse 9 may not be completely tenable because Jesus Christ also taught that we must forgive those who hurt us until we have forgiven 490 times (likely in one day).

> *Then came Peter to him, and said, Lord, how oft shall*
> *my brother sin against me, and I forgive him? till seven*
> *times? Jesus saith unto him, I say not unto thee, Until*
> *seven times: but, Until seventy times seven. So likewise*
> *shall my heavenly Father do also unto you, if ye from your*
> *hearts forgive not every one his brother their trespasses.*
> *(Matthew 18:21–22, 35)*

While I do not wish to give the impression that Jesus Christ contradicted Himself, or overlooked or forgot His teaching on forgiveness, and gave the exception just to keep couples from adultery/fornication or to create a loophole for them, I will say that He taught that every sin is forgivable except the sin of blasphemy against the Holy Spirit. He said, "Wherefore I say unto you, All manner of sin and blasphemy shall be forgiven unto men: but the blasphemy against the Holy Ghost shall not be forgiven unto men. And whosoever speaketh a word against the Son of man, it shall be forgiven him: but whosoever speaketh against the Holy Ghost, it shall not be forgiven him, neither in this world, neither in the world to come" (Matthew 12:31–32; Mark 3:28–29).

Subsequently, scripture says that if we confess our sins, the Lord, who is faithful and just, will forgive us our sins and cleanse us from all forms of unrighteousness (1 John 1:9). So, who is mankind (either husband or wife) not to forgive a fellow human whom God has or may have forgiven? When an offender repents and confesses to God (and perhaps to the offended too), why continue to insist on divorce because of what he or she did to you?

Whatever the case, couples are required to keep their marriage sacred and undefiled. As Hebrews 13:4 says, "Let marriage be held in honor among all, and let the marriage bed be undefiled, for God will judge the sexually immoral and adulterous" (ESV). God will judge. He did not ask you to do the judging on His behalf.

Marriage without Divorce

Jesus Christ discouraged divorce. He also discouraged remarriage of divorcées. A story is told of a church pastor who divorced his wife and married a woman member of his congregation who had also divorced her husband. Perhaps the pastor based his action on "one man, one wife at a time." But again the Word of God says this:

> *And he answered and said unto them, Have ye not read, that he which made them at the beginning made them male and female, And said, For this cause shall a man leave father and mother, and shall cleave to his wife: and they twain shall be one flesh? Wherefore they are no more twain, but one flesh. What therefore God hath joined together, let not man put asunder.*

> *And I say unto you, Whosoever shall put away his wife, except it be for fornication, and shall marry another, committeth adultery: and whoso marrieth her which is put away doth commit adultery. (Matthew 19:4–6, 9)*

Children Are to Honor Their Parents

The ideal family is one in which children honor their parents unconditionally "as to the Lord."

> *And he said unto him, Why callest thou me good? there is none good but one, that is, God: but if thou wilt enter into life, keep the commandments. He saith unto him,*

95

Which? Jesus said, Thou shalt do no murder, Thou shalt not commit adultery, Thou shalt not steal, Thou shalt not bear false witness, Honour thy father and thy mother: and, Thou shalt love thy neighbour as thyself. (Matthew 19:17–19)

And he said unto them, How is it that ye sought me? wist ye not that I must be about my Father's business? And they understood not the saying which he spake unto them. And he went down with them, and came to Nazareth, and was subject unto them: but his mother kept all these sayings in her heart. (Luke 2:49–51)

And he said unto them, Full well ye reject the commandment of God, that ye may keep your own tradition. For Moses said, Honour thy father and thy mother; and, Whoso curseth father or mother, let him die the death: But ye say, If a man shall say to his father or mother, It is Corban, that is to say, a gift, by whatsoever thou mightest be profited by me; he shall be free. And ye suffer him no more to do ought for his father or his mother; Making the word of God of none effect through your tradition, which ye have delivered: and many such like things do ye. (Mark 7:9–13)

Jesus saith unto her, Woman, what have I to do with thee? mine hour is not yet come. His mother saith unto the servants, Whatsoever he saith unto you, do it. And there were set there six waterpots of stone, after the manner of the purifying of the Jews, containing two or three firkins apiece. Jesus saith unto them, Fill the waterpots with water. And they filled them up to the brim. And he saith unto them, Draw out now, and bear unto the governor of the feast. And they bare it. (John 2:4–8)

Although it was not yet time for Jesus Christ to begin His ministry, yet He did as His mother desired in obedience to her and to honor her.

7.2 The Ideal Family According To The Teachings Of The Apostle Paul

The principal teachings of the apostle Paul about the ideal family, the ideal marital status, and family members' roles are found in his letters to the Corinthians, Ephesians, and Colossians. He also made some related recommendations that touch on the family to the young Pastors Timothy and Titus.

It is not certain whether the apostle Paul was ever married, divorced, or widowed. However, some scholars have tried to prove that he was either widowed or, more unlikely, divorced since he was a Pharisee and either a member or an agent of the Sanhedrin. At that level in Judaism it was expected that he should have been married. I feel though that if he was widowed or divorced, as a Christian he should never wish that all be widowed or divorced like he was. The major reason he would advise all to be married is to avoid fornication (sexual immorality), which is a sin against God and the fornicator. Paul wrote the following things:

- "It is good for a man not to touch a woman. Nevertheless, to avoid fornication, let every man have his own wife, and let every woman have her own husband" (1 Corinthians 7:1–2).
- "For I would that all men were even as I myself. But every man hath his proper gift of God, one after this manner, and another after that" (1 Corinthians 7:7).
- "Flee fornication. Every sin that a man doeth is without the body; but he that committeth fornication sinneth against his own body" (1 Corinthians 6:18).

Additionally, while forbidding divorce, the apostle Paul said:

> *And unto the married I command, yet not I, but the*
> *Lord, Let not the wife depart from her husband: But and*
> *if she depart, let her remain unmarried or be reconciled to*
> *her husband: and let not the husband put away his wife.*
> *But to the rest speak I, not the Lord: If any brother hath*
> *a wife that believeth not, and she be pleased to dwell with*
> *him, let him not put her away. The wife is bound by the*
> *law as long as her husband liveth; but if her husband be*
> *dead, she is at liberty to be married to whom she will; only*
> *in the Lord. (1 Corinthians 7:10–12, 39)*

In effect, marriage is a divinely arranged guard against sexual sin, provided that every man keeps to his wife and every wife to her husband. Paul recommends celibacy only for people who have been gifted it by God and can maintain it. "But if they cannot contain, let them marry: for it is better to marry than to burn" (1 Corinthians 7:9).

In the Epistle to the Ephesians, the apostle Paul exhorted the Church and followed that exhortation immediately with one to the family. To the Church Paul said the following:

> *Be ye therefore followers of God, as dear children; And*
> *walk in love, as Christ also hath loved us, and hath*
> *given himself for us an offering and a sacrifice to God*
> *for a sweetsmelling savour. But fornication, and all*
> *uncleanness, or covetousness, let it not be once named*
> *among you, as becometh saints; Neither filthiness, nor*
> *foolish talking, nor jesting, which are not convenient:*
> *but rather giving of thanks. For this ye know, that no*
> *whoremonger, nor unclean person, nor covetous man,*
> *who is an idolater, hath any inheritance in the kingdom*
> *of Christ and of God.*

Let no man deceive you with vain words: for because of these things cometh the wrath of God upon the children of disobedience. Be not ye therefore partakers with them. For ye were sometimes darkness, but now are ye light in the Lord: walk as children of light: (For the fruit of the Spirit is in all goodness and righteousness and truth;) Proving what is acceptable unto the Lord.

And have no fellowship with the unfruitful works of darkness, but rather reprove them. For it is a shame even to speak of those things which are done of them in secret. But all things that are reproved are made manifest by the light: for whatsoever doth make manifest is light. Wherefore he saith, Awake thou that sleepest, and arise from the dead, and Christ shall give thee light.

See then that ye walk circumspectly, not as fools, but as wise, Redeeming the time, because the days are evil. Wherefore be ye not unwise, but understanding what the will of the Lord is. And be not drunk with wine, wherein is excess; but be filled with the Spirit; Speaking to yourselves in psalms and hymns and spiritual songs, singing and making melody in your heart to the Lord; Giving thanks always for all things unto God and the Father in the name of our Lord Jesus Christ; Submitting yourselves one to another in the fear of God. (Ephesians 5:1–21)

Following this admonition to the whole Church, which ends at verse 21, the apostle addressed members of ideal families that consist of wife/mother, husband/father, children, and (where applicable) servants. In this teaching there is no provision for cohabiting persons (boyfriends/girlfriends or concubines/mistresses) or same- sex partners living together as spouses. The address reads as follows:

99

Wives, submit yourselves unto your own husbands, as unto the Lord. For the husband is the head of the wife, even as Christ is the head of the church: and he is the saviour of the body. Therefore as the church is subject unto Christ, so let the wives be to their own husbands in every thing.

Husbands, love your wives, even as Christ also loved the church, and gave himself for it; That he might sanctify and cleanse it with the washing of water by the word, That he might present it to himself a glorious church, not having spot, or wrinkle, or any such thing; but that it should be holy and without blemish. So ought men to love their wives as their own bodies. He that loveth his wife loveth himself. For no man ever yet hated his own flesh; but nourisheth and cherisheth it, even as the Lord the church: For we are members of his body, of his flesh, and of his bones. For this cause shall a man leave his father and mother, and shall be joined unto his wife, and they two shall be one flesh. This is a great mystery: but I speak concerning Christ and the church. Nevertheless let every one of you in particular so love his wife even as himself; and the wife see that she reverence her husband.

Children, obey your parents in the Lord: for this is right. Honour thy father and mother; which is the first commandment with promise; That it may be well with thee, and thou mayest live long on the earth.

And, ye fathers, provoke not your children to wrath: but bring them up in the nurture and admonition of the Lord.
Servants, be obedient to them that are your masters according to the flesh, with fear and trembling, in

singleness of your heart, as unto Christ; Not with eyeservice, as menpleasers; but as the servants of Christ, doing the will of God from the heart; With good will doing service, as to the Lord, and not to men: Knowing that whatsoever good thing any man doeth, the same shall he receive of the Lord, whether he be bond or free.

And, ye masters, do the same things unto them, forbearing threatening: knowing that your Master also is in heaven; neither is there respect of persons with him. (Ephesians 5:22–6:9)

The teaching in this passage is meant to have two major effects:

— to exemplify or typify the mystery of the relationship between Jesus Christ and His Church (His bride) (vv. 23–24)
— to explain the principles that the ideal family should adopt and practice in order to portray the Jesus Christ–Church relationship

Wives

Wives should submit (be submissive) to their husbands as to the Lord because the husband is the head of the wife, even as Christ is the head of the Church: and He is the Savior of the body (vv. 22 and 23). An adage says that a fully submissive wife fully controls the heart of her husband.

Some synonyms of *submissive* are *obedient, compliant, unassertive*, and *yielding*. While the God's Word Translation (GWT) of the Bible renders verse 22 thus: "Wives, place yourselves under your husbands' authority as you have placed yourselves under the Lord's authority," the Contemporary English Version (CEV) puts it thus: "A wife should put her husband first, as she does the Lord."

In this admonition, the phrase "as unto the Lord" is very

important. The *Cambridge Bible for Schools and Colleges* comments on it as follows: "[As unto the Lord] Who is, in a peculiar sense, represented to the wife by the husband. In wifely submission to him she not only acts on the general principle of the acceptance of the Will of God expressed in circumstances: she sees in that attitude a special reflection, as it were, of her relations to the Lord Himself. Her attitude has a special sanction thus from Him"[4]

In the same vein, *Barnes' Notes on the Bible* comments on the phrase, saying, "As unto the Lord—As you would to the Lord, because the Lord requires it, and has given to the husband this authority."[5]

The apostle Paul similarly wrote the same instructions to wives in his epistles to the Colossians, Timothy, and Titus: "Wives, submit yourselves unto your own husbands, as it is fit in the Lord" (Colossians 3:18). This is part of the Colossians passage (3:18–4:1) that is parallel to Ephesians 5:21–6:9, both of which address the ideal total Christian family:

- "That they may teach the young women to be sober, to love their husbands, to love their children, To be discreet, chaste, keepers at home, good, obedient to their own husbands, that the word of God be not blasphemed" (Titus 2:4–5).
- "Let the woman learn in silence with all subjection" (1 Timothy 2:11).
- "But I would have you know, that the head of every man is Christ; and the head of the woman is the man; and the head of Christ is God. For the man is not of the woman: but the woman of the man. Neither was the man created for the woman; but the woman for the man" (1 Corinthians 11:3, 8–9).

---

[4] "As unto the Lord," accessed July 8, 2018,
http://biblehub.com/commentaries/cambridge/ephesians/5-22.htm.
[5] "As unto the Lord," accessed July 8, 2018,
http://biblehub.com/commentaries/barnes/ephesians/5.htm.

Some feminist preachers and teachers merge Ephesians 5:21 (above), which closes the apostle's admonition to the Church, with the admonition to the family that commences at verse 22. On the basis of this merger, such preachers claim that husband and wife should *submit to each other*, forgetting, or ignoring, that in verse 21 the scripture addresses one to another (implying a group of more than two persons—the church in this case). If the apostle had meant verse 21 for husband and wife, he would most likely have said to "submit to each other." It should also be noted that verse 21 is a continuation of the idea that starts at verse 18, as follows:

> *And be not drunk with wine, wherein is excess; but be filled with the Spirit; Speaking to yourselves in psalms and hymns and spiritual songs, singing and making melody in your heart to the Lord; Giving thanks always for all things unto God and the Father in the name of our Lord Jesus Christ; Submitting yourselves one to another in the fear of God. (Ephesians 5:18–21)*

Some feminist preachers and some theologians are of the opinion that the hierarchical family structure recommended in Ephesians 5:22–6:9 negates or contradicts the statement in Galatians 3:28 that says, "There is neither Jew nor Greek, there is neither bond nor free, there is neither male nor female: for ye are all one in Christ Jesus," and that reflected the (now obsolete) Greco-Roman culture of those days. They claim that Paul's exhortations on submission were to accommodate the culture in a way to make doubtful the ruling authorities' suspicion of such new religious movements that preached equality of all men.[6] Meanwhile, if this idea were true, it would have left the apostle Paul a hypocrite. However, Moo suggests that the instructions on household code did not simply reflect the prevailing culture at the time, even though they were obviously directed toward

---

[6] Douglas J. Moo, *The Letters to the Colossians and to Philemon* (Grand Rapids, MI: William B. Eerdmans, 2008), 294–95.

the prevailing culture (e.g., because it also addressed slavery), and as such "they must be 'heard' as an authentic New Testament voice, integrated with, and not simply overridden by, the very important insistence on 'equality' in Christ."[7]

William Barclay, commenting on Titus 2:3–5 (partly quoted above), believed that the exhortation was temporary considering that the respectable woman of the ancient Greek world lived a secluded life and was mostly homebound, and if such women in the early Church "burst every limitation" on the basis of equality of all in Christ, it would have brought discredit to the Church and would have made the world say that the Church had corrupted womanhood. Barclay concludes, however, that homemaking is an unequaled career (for wives) and that "it is infinitely more important that a mother should be at home to put her children to bed and hear them say their prayers than that she should attend all the public and church meetings in the world."[8]

A wife who does not believe in submitting to and respecting her husband is disobedient and may not be able to confidently teach her children to respect their father, or if she were, her teaching would be hypocritical and ineffective because children learn more by emulating than from instructions. That negatively affects society.

Husbands

> *Husbands, love your wives, even as Christ also loved the church, and gave himself for it; 26 That he might sanctify and cleanse it with the washing of water by the word, 27 That he might present it to himself a glorious church, not having spot, or wrinkle, or any such thing; but that it should be holy and without blemish. 28 So ought men*

---

[7] Moo, *The Letters to the Colossians*, 294–95.

[8] William Barclay, *The Letters to Timothy, Titus, and Philemon* (Philadelphia: Westminster Press, 1975), 250–51.

to love their wives as their own bodies. He that loveth his
wife loveth himself. (Ephesians 5:25–28)

The parallel passage in Colossians 3:19 simply says, "Husbands, love your wives, and be not bitter against them." This appears too simple a responsibility for a husband to whom the wife should be subject in all things until you study the implications of the kind of love Jesus has for the Church, to the extent of physically giving His life for the Church.

Husbands are required to love their wives like Jesus Christ loved the Church, to the extent of giving His life for the Church. The kind of love Jesus Christ has for the Church, for which He gave His all (His life), is very demanding, compelling, and involving. It is the agape kind of love, giving without expecting to receive in return. The responsibilities carried by this requirement on husbands (of wives who should "submit unto their husbands in all things as to the Lord"), are enormous. These responsibilities include

- sanctifying and cleansing her (Ephesians 5:26);
- ensuring she has not spot, or wrinkle, or any such thing; but that she should be holy and without blemish (Ephesians 5:27);
- loving wives as [the men's] own bodies (Ephesians 5:28); and
- nourishing and cherishing her, even as the Lord [nourishes and cherishes] the Church (Ephesians 5:29).

Furthermore, the requirement of the husband has limitations because he is head of the family, as noted by *Barnes' Notes on the Bible*:

In everything, except that which relates to "conscience and religion," [the husband] has authority. But there his authority ceases. He has no right to require [his wife] to commit an act of dishonesty, to connive at wrongdoing, to

> *visit a place of amusement which her conscience tells her*
> *is wrong, nor has he a right to interfere with the proper*
> *discharge of her religious duties. He has no right to forbid*
> *her to go to church at the proper and usual time, or to*
> *make a profession of religion when she pleases. He has*
> *no right to forbid her endeavoring to exercise a religious*
> *influence over her children, or to endeavor to lead them*
> *to God. She is bound to obey God, rather than any man*
> *[as per Acts 4:19].[9]*

"While, however, it is to be conceded that the husband has "authority" over the wife and a "right" to command in all cases that do not pertain to the conscience, it should be remarked as follows:

1. His command should be reasonable and proper.
2. He has no right to require anything wrong or contrary to the will of God."[10]

Children and Fathers

> *Children,[11] obey your parents in the Lord: for this is*
> *right. Honour thy father and mother; which is the first*
> *commandment with promise; That it may be well with thee,*
> *and thou mayest live long on the earth. (Ephesians 6:1–3)*

In the ideal family, children are to obey their parents unconditionally. This requirement helps to promote long life, all things being equal as the economist would say. And just as wives,

---

[9] "But Peter and John answered and said unto them, Whether it be right in the sight of God to hearken unto you more than unto God, judge ye" (Acts 4:19).

[10] Ephesians 5:22, Accessed July 8, 2018, http://biblehub.com/commentaries/barnes/ephesians/5.htm.

[11] *Children* here include adult children and younger children below the age of accountability.

children are to obey their parents in the Lord. This implies that there are a few conditions under which a child could be disobedient to his or her parents and be justified. Jesus Christ said, "But whosoever shall deny me before men, him will I also deny before my Father which is in heaven. Think not that I am come to send peace on earth: I came not to send peace, but a sword. For I am come to set a man at variance against his father, and the daughter against her mother, and the daughter in law against her mother in law" (Matthew 10:33–35).

Just like in the husband's relationship to his wife, the parent has no right to require the child to commit an act of dishonesty or to connive at wrongdoing. The child is bound to obey God, not any man [or woman], when he becomes accountable. It is only on such grounds that a child can justifiably disobey parents. This is the way Jesus Christ will cause a child to be at variance or odds with his or her parent.

Immediately following the instruction to the children, the apostle says to fathers,[12] "And, ye fathers, provoke not your children to wrath: but bring them up in the nurture and admonition of the Lord" (Ephesians 6:4; Colossians 3:21). While the *New International Version* commentary on this explains provocation to anger as a parental discipline to the point of exasperation,[13] causing children to sin should be seen as a way of provoking them. Remember that they are admonished to obey their parents *in the Lord* (Ephesians 6:1). Jesus Christ had earlier taught that it was pitiable for anyone to cause children to sin:

- "But whoso shall offend one of these little ones which believe in me, it were better for him that a millstone were hanged

---

[12] *Children* here include adult children and younger children below the age of accountability. However, in the context of this exhortation, Dr. Moo says the Greek word πατερες (*pateres*) translated in Colossians 3:21 as "fathers" can also mean both parents. Moo, *The Letters to the Colossians,* 306.

[13] *Life Application Study Bible* (*NIV*), 1990.

about his neck, and that he were drowned in the depth of the sea" (Matthew 18:6).

- "And whosoever shall offend one of these little ones that believe in me, it is better for him that a millstone were hanged about his neck, and he were cast into the sea" (Mark 9:42).
- "It were better for him that a millstone were hanged about his neck, and he cast into the sea, than that he should offend one of these little ones" (Luke 17:2).

It is the responsibility of a Christian father, under normal circumstances, to provide for his family. Failure to do so implies that he has denied the faith and is worse than an unbeliever (1 Timothy 5:8). It is required of a father to rule his household to ensure that his children are well-behaved. Though this is a requirement of men aspiring for the office of deacon or pastor/bishop, it behooves every father to discharge this responsibility since, who knows, one may be called into those ministries at some time.

> *This is a true saying, if a man desire the office of a bishop, he desireth a good work. A bishop then must be blameless, the husband of one wife, vigilant, sober, of good behaviour, given to hospitality, apt to teach; Not given to wine, no striker, not greedy of filthy lucre; but patient, not a brawler, not covetous; One that ruleth well his own house, having his children in subjection with all gravity; (For if a man know not how to rule his own house, how shall he take care of the church of God?). (1 Timothy 3:1–5; emphasis added)*

In Paul's letter to young Pastor Titus, he gave instructions similar to those he gave Timothy (quoted immediately above), as follows: "For this cause left I thee in Crete, that thou shouldest set in order the things that are wanting, and ordain elders in every city, as

I had appointed thee: If any be blameless, the husband of one wife, having faithful children not accused of riot or unruly" (Titus 1:5–6).

Servants[14]

> *Servants, be obedient to them that are your masters according to the flesh, with fear and trembling, in singleness of your heart, as unto Christ; Not with eyeservice, as menpleasers; but as the servants of Christ, doing the will of God from the heart; With good will doing service, as to the Lord, and not to men: Knowing that whatsoever good thing any man doeth, the same shall he receive of the Lord, whether he be bond or free. (Ephesians 6:5–8)*

> *Servants, obey in all things your masters according to the flesh; not with eyeservice, as menpleasers; but in singleness of heart, fearing God; And whatsoever ye do, do it heartily, as to the Lord, and not unto men; Knowing that of the Lord ye shall receive the reward of the inheritance: for ye serve the Lord Christ. But he that doeth wrong shall receive for the wrong which he hath done: and there is no respect of persons. (Colossians 3:22–25)*

Ordinarily, the nuclear family is composed of husband, wife, and children. But in the Greco-Roman world, households included domestic slaves who rendered services to the family. Similarly, in some contemporary developing nations, servants (usually children of underprivileged parents), who may be paid in cash or in kind, also live with, and constitute part of, the family. In some African

---

[14] The Greek δοῦλος (*doulos*) means in English "slave" or "servant." Though the Greek word for "employee" is υπάλληλος (*ypállilos*), the admonition to servants/slaves does well to refer to employees at any level.

families, some kindhearted parents help their good servants to learn a trade or go through formal education like their children.

The ideal family is one in which servants (or, previously, slaves)—where present—should be genuinely obedient to their masters in all things, bearing in mind that their employment is in service to Christ, and more so, such servants/slaves who are Christians have a common Master (Jesus Christ) with their earthly masters. The slaves should serve with singleness of heart and with fear of God.

Masters[15]

> *And, ye masters, do the same things unto them, forbearing threatening: knowing that your Master also is in heaven; neither is there respect of persons with him. (Ephesians 6:9)*

> *Masters, give unto your servants that which is just and equal; knowing that ye also have a Master in heaven. (Colossians 4:1)*

The ideal masters should deal with their servants/slaves in the fear of God without threatening them, bearing in mind that it is the same God who created the masters who created the slaves (in God's image). Both the masters and the slaves serve the same Lord via their peculiar services. Masters are, therefore, to be fair and just in dealing with their slaves/servants/employees. Commenting on Colossians 4:1 (quoted above), Moo, citing Peter T. O'Brien, says that Paul might have implied that masters should treat their slaves in the right way, "that is, treat them with scrupulous fairness."[16] Moo

---

[15] The master here is the husband of the wife discussed earlier; he is the father of the children and head of the household. He is a master here with the presence of a slave/servant in the household. The term *master* is safely applicable to an employer whose employee is in a servant relationship with him.

[16] Moo, *The Letters to the Colossians*, 317.

further noted that Christian slave owners need to remember that they are answerable to a higher Master, the Lord Jesus.[17]

There are Old Testament laws regarding masters and their paid servants, to which both Jesus Christ and Paul referred. Consider what is said of this subject in the Old Testament:

- "Thou shalt not defraud thy neighbour, neither rob him: the wages of him that is hired shall not abide with thee all night until the morning" (Leviticus 19:13).
- "At his day thou shalt give him his hire, neither shall the sun go down upon it; for he is poor, and setteth his heart upon it: lest he cry against thee unto the Lord, and it be sin unto thee" (Deuteronomy 24:15).

Speaking on this topic, Jesus Christ said the following:

- "For the workman is worthy of his meat" (Matthew 10:10b).
- "And in the same house remain, eating and drinking such things as they give: *for the labourer is worthy of his hire*" (Luke 10:7a; emphasis added).

Paul cited the law as follows: "For the scripture saith, thou shalt not muzzle the ox that treadeth out the corn. And, *The labourer is worthy of his reward*" (1 Timothy 5:18; emphasis added).

To conclude this section, the comments of the NIV Bible on Colossians 4:1 read, "Christian employees should do their jobs as if Jesus Christ were their supervisor. And Christian employers should treat their employees fairly and with respect."[18]

---

[17] Moo, *The Letters to the Colossians*, 317.

[18] *Life Application Bible (NIV)*, 2014.

7.3 The Ideal Family According To The Teachings Of The Apostle Peter

The First Epistle of Peter was addressed to the brethren—Christians in diaspora. Its purpose was to offer encouragement to brethren facing suffering as stated in chapter 5:12, as follows: "I have written briefly, exhorting, and testifying that this is the true grace of God wherein ye stand." It was to assure believers that, in spite of what they pass through, faith in Christ is where the true grace of God is found. It was meant to boost the confidence of believers.

The apostle had dealt with different issues in the preceding passages, digressing in chapter 3 to address the family, thus:

> *Likewise, ye wives, be in subjection to your own husbands; that, if any obey not the word, they also may without the word be won by the conversation of the wives; While they behold your chaste conversation coupled with fear. Whose adorning let it not be that outward adorning of plaiting the hair, and of wearing of gold, or of putting on of apparel; But let it be the hidden man of the heart, in that which is not corruptible, even the ornament of a meek and quiet spirit, which is in the sight of God of great price. For after this manner in the old time the holy women also, who trusted in God, adorned themselves, being in subjection unto their own husbands: Even as Sara obeyed Abraham, calling him lord: whose daughters ye are, as long as ye do well, and are not afraid with any amazement.*
>
> *Likewise, ye husbands, dwell with them according to knowledge, giving honour unto the wife, as unto the weaker vessel, and as being heirs together of the grace of life; that your prayers be not hindered. (1 Peter 3:1–7)*

This passage addresses wives and husbands. It assumes that an ideal family consists of a wife and her husband. Though children are not mentioned, it is assumed there are children. Similarly, the apostle Peter has not included servants in the family as Paul did in his epistles to the Ephesians and Colossians. Peter earlier addressed servants in chapter 2, admonishing them to be submissive to their masters, as follows: "Servants, be subject to your masters with all fear; not only to the good and gentle, but also to the froward. For this is thankworthy, if a man for conscience toward God endure grief, suffering wrongfully. For what glory is it, if, when ye be buffeted for your faults, ye shall take it patiently? but if, when ye do well, and suffer for it, ye take it patiently, this is acceptable with God" (1 Peter 2:18–20).

The admonition in 1 Peter 3:1 to the family begins with *likewise,* that is, in the same manner (of submissiveness), wives should be subject to their own husbands. This is because their humility and reverent demeanor would touch the hearts of husbands who would otherwise refuse to believe the gospel. Verses 5 and 6 are noteworthy:

> *For after this manner in the old time the holy women also, who trusted in God, adorned themselves, being in subjection unto their own husbands: Even as Sara obeyed Abraham, calling him lord: whose daughters ye are, as long as ye do well, and are not afraid with any amazement. (1 Peter 3:5–6)*

The second part of this admonition is to husbands:

> *Likewise, ye husbands, dwell with them according to knowledge, giving honour unto the wife, as unto the weaker vessel, and as being heirs together of the grace of life; that your prayers be not hindered. (1 Peter 3:7)*

By this, husbands are required to do the following things:

(1) Dwell with their wives *according to knowledge*. Husbands should live with their wives. For husbands to live with their wives excludes marriage from a distance. But the phrase "according to knowledge" is the part of the requirement that is difficult to explain. *Vincent's Word Studies in the New Testament* simply states it as "with an intelligent recognition of the nature of the marriage relation."[19]

Matthew Poole's Commentary on the Holy Bible suggests two possible interpretations:

Either "according to that knowledge of the Divine will, which by the gospel ye have obtained" or "prudently and wisely, and as becomes those that understand their duty."[20] Similarly, Guy N. Woods says it implies "with due understanding of the nature of the marital relation, each showing proper regard for the other, and both discharging the duties peculiarly theirs."[21]

(2) *Honor their wives.* Some synonyms of *honor* are *esteem, admire, appreciate, respect, value,* and *cherish.* Husbands should cherish and appreciate their wives and not despise them or treat them like slaves. Further reference can be made to Paul's teaching to the Ephesians, where he said, "Husbands, love your wives, even as Christ also loved the church, and gave himself for it; So ought men to love their wives as their own bodies. He that loveth his wife loveth himself. For no man ever yet hated his own flesh; but

---

[19] 1 Peter 3:7, Accessed August 5, 2018, https://biblehub.com/commentaries/ vws/1_peter/3.htm.

[20] Accessed August 5, 2018, https://biblehub.com/commentaries/poole/1_peter/3.htm.

[21] Guy N. Woods, *A Commentary on the New Testament Epistles of Peter, John, and Jude* (Nashville, TN: Gospel Advocate, 1973), 92.

nourisheth and cherisheth it, even as the Lord the church" (Ephesians 5:25, 28–29).

(3) As to *the weaker vessel*—this implies the wife "being" or "being like" the vessel, less strong physically in comparison to the husband. Woods, like Walvoord and Zuck,[22] comments that the reason a woman is referred to as the weaker vessel is not because of her moral or intellectual inferiority to the man but because of her lack of the kind of physical capacity or dexterity inherent in, or that characterizes, the male.[23]

(4) And as to *being heirs together of the grace of life*—another reason husbands must give honor to their wives is that the wives, being Christians too (bearing in mind that the Epistle of Peter was addressed to Christians in diaspora), are co-recipients of the saving grace of God in Christ Jesus. Romans 8:16–17 says, "The Spirit itself beareth witness with our spirit, that we are the children of God: And if children, then heirs; heirs of God, and joint-heirs with Christ; if so be that we suffer with him, that we may be also glorified together."

(5) *So that [their] prayers be not hindered.* Lack of fellowship between husband and wife arising from the man's failure to care for his wife or the woman's failure to play her part as described is capable of hindering the prayers of the family. *The Pulpit Commentary* agrees: "If husband and wife live together without mutual reverence and affection, there can be no sympathy in united prayer; the promise made by Christ in Matthew 18:19 cannot be realized. Nor can either pray acceptably if they live at variance."[24]

---

[22] John F. Walvoord and Roy B. Zuck, eds., *The Bible Knowledge Commentary: Epistles and Prophecy* (Colorado Springs: David C. Cook, 1983, 2018), 87.

[23] Woods, *A Commentary*, 93.

[24] 1 Peter 3 Accessed August 6, 2018, https://biblehub.com/commentaries/pulpit/1_peter/3.htm.

Matthew 18:19 reads, "Again I say unto you, That if two of you shall agree on earth as touching any thing that they shall ask, it shall be done for them of my Father which is in heaven."

Although Jesus directed this to the Church (in His disciples), it is also applicable to the Christian couple.

Certainly the subjects of these admonitions of Peter tend to be opposed to the demands and beliefs of the women's liberation movement. This is especially true with regard to wives' submission to their husbands and with husbands seeing their wives as the weaker sex no matter what the reason. One woman has said that what a man can do, a woman can also do, and do even better. But the admonitions are in the inspired Word of God. Hence it is an occasion of wisdom to follow and obey.

CHAPTER 8

EFFECTS OF SINGLE PARENTING BY CHOICE

SINGLE PARENTING GENERALLY HAS ADVERSE EFFECTS on the children, the parents, and society. It is understandable when it results from an "act of God"—circumstances beyond one's control. But for one to be party to, contributor to, or the cause of the situation that ends in single parenting does not incur the blessings of God. Bearing in mind that God is not the author of confusion or disorder (1 Corinthians 14:33), but of peace, He will not leave unjudged anyone who brings disorder to His creation. Since a greater percentage of single parents arise from separation and divorce, we shall consider here the effects of single parenting arising from divorce.

8.1 Effects Of Single Parenting On The Children

1. The events that lead to the separation or divorce of the parents do traumatize the children. And in order to win the favor and sympathy of the children, the parent who has custody of the children more often than not feeds them with terribly painted pictures of the other parent. This is especially true if the children are very young at the time of the separation.

    This situation is worse when the mother has custody of the children. The children become so sympathetic with their mom that they hate their divorced dad with a passion. They really become filled with resentment in consequence of the ugly memories.

2. Oftentimes other problems arise from the issue of custody of the children. The children are required to be periodically picked by, or taken to, the parent who does not have custody of them. This has some negative effects on the children's regular flow of activities. The children are fed with different information about their other parent, causing a conflict in their minds. This becomes worse if the two divorced parents belong to different religions. Take, for example, a couple who divorced after the woman converted to Christianity from Islam, and she has custody of their two sons, aged about eight and five years at the time of the divorce. The father takes the boys at weekends and during the holidays. You can imagine what the boys go through. It would be difficult for them to choose which religion to belong to.

    A true-life story, *A Mother's Love*, told to typify the great love of God for those who trust in Him, tells us that Sue was young when her parents divorced, and the outcome of the legal tussle for Sue's legal custody and other related matters was that Sue was sent to a children's home for a while, where bigger children bullied her. This caused her to feel lonely and abandoned. While she hardly saw her father, her mother visited her only once a month. Her mother told her many years later that it was the rules of the home that restricted the frequency of her visits, in view of which she would stand behind the fence of the home to catch a glimpse of her daughter.[1]

The question is, what did Sue do to deserve all that punishment from her parents, who seemed to have loved her? Should these parents have continued to inflict the torture on her and on themselves?

3. Depending on which of the two parents is absent from the home, the father figure or mother figure, as the case may be, may become completely lost to the children's character. This means that the children become too feminine or too masculine, as the case may be, in character. When character structure tilts too conspicuously to one side without a balance, something definitely goes awry.

4. The children may be denied some parental care or benefits when the custodial parent has to choose between work and caring for them, leading to child neglect.

5. The children may not be properly disciplined at home since the single parent might have too much to be preoccupied with, thereby leaving child discipline to a third party such as the children's teachers and/or nannies and other household helpers.

6. Child-rearing at home may actually fall more to nannies and other household helpers. Since the one who pays the piper dictates the tune, the characters of the children, more often than not, may be molded after the household helpers or nannies. The household helpers have no serious commitment and, because of this, leave the children to

---

[1] Leslie Koh, *Our Daily Bread* (Grand Rapids, MI: Our Daily Bread Ministries, 2018).

do what they please, or else they overcontrol the children, which could lead to abuse. On the other hand, the reaction of the children's parent to the household helpers when the children report the help contributes to the kind of attention the help gives the children in the absence of the parent.

7. Financial resources for a one-parent family may be insufficient, unlike those of a two-parent family; hence children from a single-parent family may lack sufficient resources for education, health care, and other forms of care.

8. Children may begin bearing family responsibilities too soon in order to fill the gap left by the other parent. They may be subjected to child labor.

9. Children of single-parent homes are more likely to drop out of school, end up in jail, or become pregnant as teens.

10. It appears more difficult for such children to leave home for extracurricular activities or to socialize because of the help and company they give their parent at home. The advantageous side of this negative aspect is that the children may not get involved with bad friends outside the home.

11. The children may have causes to admire and/or envy children from families with both a father and a mother.

12. Such children being brought up by single parents may suffer psychological effects such as depression, hatred, sadism, and suspicion, among other behavioral disturbances, which could make them vulnerable to addiction to drugs and alcoholism, as well as teenage pregnancy and even suicide.

13. They are more likely to have broken homes themselves when they become adults, or they may choose to remain single for life. Some single parents, especially mothers, overprotect their sons, and the love and company that exists between them, to the extent that their relationship adversely affects their daughters-in-law later. In other words, the relationship interferes with the relationships of their sons with their wives.

8.2 Effects of Single Parenting on the Parents Themselves

People who choose to become and remain single parents also, like their children, suffer some adverse effects from the decision. These are two people who used to see something good and lovely in each other. It is hurtful to part ways.

Much as they enjoy freedom—not being accountable to anyone on matters concerning their families—they face difficulties and issues that traditional mother–father families are faced with. This is not to say that the latter do not have problems. But God gives them the grace to cope with and surmount such problems if they remain faithful and trust God to help them.

The effects of single parenting by choice on the parents may vary depending on how the choice arises. For instance, the single parent who never lived as a married spouse with the other parent of the child may not suffer the effects that are suffered by divorced parents. The following are a few of the effects on parents of single parenting by choice:

(1) The parents suffer some degree of shock and require a period of time to adjust to the new status. This is applicable no matter which of the parents initiates the divorce proceedings. However, the intensity of the shock may vary.

(2) Being a father and mother at the same time (that is, to play the roles of both parents by oneself), having to meet the demands that both parents should normally provide, is stressful. The single parent has to do planning, financing, and executing of all plans for the family. This could lead to emotional stress and gradually lead to the nervous breakdown of the parent.

(3) Problems are likely to arise from the issue of custody of the children. This is in view of the fact that the parent who does not have custody may be allotted times for visiting or seeing the children or to take them to his or her home

for a specified length of time and then return them. The schedules for this could be affected by other personal activities including work and by natural phenomena such as rain, snow, or hurricane.

(4) The parent who has custody may become so seriously attached to the children that leaving home for social engagements becomes a tall order for this parent and the children. This is largely because the parent depends on the children for company and support.

(5) The parent may depend on household help for bringing up the children since the parent may need to go out to work or meet some outside engagement. The dangers inherent in this are enormous and vary according to the age(s) of the child(ren) and the gender of the child(ren) in relation to the age and gender of the household help. Certainly the household help becomes either a positive role model or a dangerous role model to the children.

(6) It may become difficult to maintain discipline in the home. The resultant effect of this on the parents, the children, and society cannot be overemphasized, as charity begins at home. A child ill-disciplined at home certainly can hardly be controlled outside the home.

(7) If the parent does not remarry and the children see him or her relating with different people of the opposite sex, that parent constitutes a bad example of morality for the children. Children learn more and faster from parents' actions than from what the parents say. The parent may, on the other hand, have to play hide-and-seek in order not to expose the children early in life to an immoral lifestyle. That too is dishonesty or hypocrisy.

(8) Occasionally the parent may suffer embarrassment when the children ask such questions as the following:
    o "Mommy, who [or where] is my daddy?"
    o "Dad, is this my new mom??

> o "Why does Dad [or Mom, as the case may be] not live with us?"
>
> o "Why do we not all live together like the family of [another child's name]?"

(9) In view of this barrage of questions, a parent may occasionally be dishonest in order to consistently please an inquisitive child.

(10) The parent may suffer loneliness. Notwithstanding the presence of the children, loneliness gradually sets in. The children do not fill the vacuum in the heart of a divorced spouse. Only a spouse does.

8.3 Effects of Single Parenting on The Society At Large And The Church

Just as single parenting by choice has some adverse effects on the parents and the children, some of which may not be quantifiable or apparent, it also has effects both on the society at large in general and the Church in particular. It is a problem for the Church especially because it has become a significant contributor to the influence of the world system on the Church. With the growth of the population of single parents by choice in society, the Church also suffers the impact, to the extent that preachers hardly preach against the phenomenon, and it has gradually become a norm rather than the exception.

Some of the many effects on the society and the Church are as follows:

1) Indiscipline that is prevalent in the home of the single-parent-by-choice family is extended to society. The adage "Charity begins at home" applies here too. Unruly behaviors and disrespect, if not easily checked at home, are extended to society outside the home. This leads to an increase in juvenile delinquencies and an increase in the incarceration of

young people with its attendant problems and consequences. Unfortunately, though, many young minority people in the USA today do not see much wrong in going to prison. Even though it is a stigma to be an ex-convict, they are not ashamed to be seen as such, especially because the society begins to prepare such minority children for prison early in life. Hence they don't mind going to and returning to prison, where there is free food, a free home, and free everything except liberty.

2) Several sociologists believe that criminal activities are more likely or more prevalent for children brought up by people who have chosen to be single parents. This is largely the result of the deficient training the children receive at home.

3) Poor parent–child communication at home usually gets carried into society and public life. The Bible says, "Let your speech be always with grace, seasoned with salt, that ye may know how ye ought to answer every man" (Colossians 4:6). When graceful speech is deficient in the home, it flows into society, since society is made up of people from the homes of families who naturally project their good characters.

4) The high rate of criminal activity produces societal unrest, fear, and anxiety and results in a lack of peace.

5) Single parenting by choice promotes an abuse of freedom, which feminism has created, and leads to debasement and "commonization" of the sex act. Sex is no longer treated as sacred.

6) Because of their low income, many single parents, especially single mothers, are likely to depend on government resources. Some people might ask whether it really matters if one must depend on the government to survive. Dependence on government is the same as depending on welfare. Some disadvantages of such dependence are discussed below.

Dependence on welfare implies relying for long periods of time on government resources for income for the purpose of meeting daily or regular basic needs like rent, food, clothing, education of children, and health care. In the United States of America, state and federal governments provide Temporary Assistance for Needy Families (TANF), food stamps (officially known as the Supplemental Nutrition Assistance Program [SNAP]), and Supplemental Security Income (SSI). The Unites States Department of Housing and Urban Development manages the programs of Section 8, the popular nickname for Section 8 of the Housing Act of 1937, which authorizes the payment of rental housing assistance to private landlords on behalf of low-income households.

Generally people who qualify to benefit from these welfare schemes are families/households living below, at, or around the poverty line. Such resources are mostly available in the Western world. Most developing nations do not have such welfare schemes.

The welfare programs are financed with taxpayer money and are operated with certain restrictions, depending on the political party in power. One of the characteristics of the beneficiaries— the dependants—is that they live mainly in projects, where their neighbors are principally people at similar poverty levels. It becomes kind of "an association of poverty-stricken people," to whom government pays little or no development attention, especially as most of such people belong to the minority races and groups.

Many children born into such environments do not aspire beyond the scope of their environment. They are often likely to live like their parent(s) did, and so the poverty cycle continues.

Dependence on welfare limits availability of income for certain needs not provided by the welfare schemes. As a result, children of such dependents are easily lured into crime, prostitution with its attendant problems such as disease and teenage pregnancy, drug use, and alcohol use.

Paul Winfree, in his article "How Welfare Spending Hurts the People It's Supposed to Help," says that when welfare is generous to able-bodied adults without any obligation to work, it undermines the motivation and need for such dependents to work and support themselves. He also argues that because there are nonfinancial benefits derived from working, such as building long-lasting relationships, the fact that welfare does not encourage working may have long-term adverse consequences.[2] Although the article cited appears to have some political undertone aimed at discrediting the work of a past administration, there is some truth in the ideas presented with regard to dependence on welfare.

Single parenting by choice impacts society by influencing decisions made by the products of such families. Such persons do not have as much sympathy, love, and feelings for family as products of complete families, especially in families where the single parents are mothers.

---

[2] Paul Winfree,"How Welfare Spending Hurts the People It's Supposed to Help," *The Daily Signal,* August 1, 2015, https://www.dailysignal.com/2015/08/01/ how-welfare-spending-hurts-the-people-its-supposed-to-help/.

CHAPTER 9

CONCLUSIONS AND RECOMMENDATIONS

9.1 Young People

As pointed out earlier, God, who created mankind and all things, said it is not good for the man to be alone, in spite of the presence of all kinds and sizes of animals around him. God then took steps to make a helpmeet fit for him. He came up with the solution to man's loneliness, a woman.

In effect, the true solution to the loneliness of any man is a woman, and vice versa. For every man, therefore, there is a woman fit for him. Conversely, for every woman, there is a man for whom she should be a helpmeet. It is only a wise man who prayerfully searches for God's appointed helpmeet for him, and a wise woman who prayerfully expects and patiently waits for the man whose "missing rib" she is. Every young man and woman should desire to get married some day at God's appointed time.

As it was not good at creation for mankind to be alone, so it is today. Since loneliness leads to, or is breeding ground for, different forms of evil thoughts and actions such as bestiality, homosexuality, fornication, murder, and suicide, it is recommended that young people be taught, as soon as they begin to be conscious of themselves and their sexes, to begin to pray for God's leading to His right/ appointed spouse for them. They should endeavor to avoid trial marriage but rather go into marriage by faith in the Lord, bearing in mind that marriage is for adults and mature-minded persons—not for kids!

> *[Marriage] is commended in the Scriptures to be honorable among all, and therefore is not by any to be entered into unadvisedly or lightly, but reverently, discreetly, advisedly, soberly and in the fear of God.*[1]

Remember, your boyfriend is not your husband! Your girlfriend is not your wife! This kind of friendship has no commitment. And let not anyone who has lost his or her marriage persuade you against going into your own marriage. God instituted marriage, and if you go into it holding onto His hands, your marriage will succeed and will be peaceful and joyful. You must determine to make it work, trusting God to help you.

9.2 Unmarried Or Cohabiting Parents

The difference between a married couple and a cohabiting couple is that while the former have the authority of their parents and the state, the latter live together as friends and begin to bear children by way of fornication. Without any fear of being judgmental, I can say that by the standards of the Holy Scriptures, such a couple lives

---

[1] *The Pastor's Handbook*, rev. ed. (Chicago: Wing Spread, 2006), 45.

in sin. Before this dispensation of grace (also known as the Church age), fornication and adultery were sins carrying immediate terrible consequences, including death.

For example, the law says the following things:

- "And the man that committeth adultery with another man's wife, even he that committeth adultery with his neighbour's wife, the adulterer and the adulteress shall surely be put to death" (Leviticus 20:10).
- "If a man meets a virgin who is not betrothed, and seizes her and lies with her, and they are found, then the man who lay with her shall give to the father of the young woman fifty shekels of silver, and she shall be his wife, because he has violated her. He may not divorce her all his days" (Deuteronomy 22:28–29 ESV).

Being under grace does not in the least imply that God has lowered His standards. It only implies that the law (of Moses) demands human beings to perform works of righteousness and demonstrates that violation of God's law separates the perpetrator from God. Furthermore, "Whosoever committeth sin transgresseth also the law: for sin is the transgression of the law" (1 John 3:4). In this dispensation of grace, God has simplified the way of redemption and salvation by giving His sinless Son, Jesus Christ, by whose righteousness mankind can be saved. Salvation does not depend on your works of righteousness (Titus 3:4–5) but on the righteousness that God gives to mankind through our faith in Christ Jesus. For the law was given by Moses, but grace and truth came by Jesus Christ (John 1:17). Grace is unmerited favor (of God), which can be, and is often, abused. Citing Jude 4, "For there are certain men crept in unawares, who were before of old ordained to this condemnation, ungodly men, turning the grace of our God into lasciviousness, and denying the only Lord God, and our Lord Jesus Christ)," Jerry Bridges says, "We abuse grace when we think we can sin and then receive forgiveness by claiming 1 John 1:9. We abuse grace when, after sinning we dwell on the compassion and mercy of God to the exclusion of His holiness and hatred of sin."[2]

Jesus Christ said, "Think not that I am come to destroy the law, or the prophets: I am not come to destroy, but to fulfil" (Matthew 5:17). So unless you repent, God still holds you accountable for every sin. The scriptures say, "Now the works of the flesh are manifest, which are these; adultery, fornication, uncleanness, lasciviousness, idolatry, witchcraft, hatred, variance, emulations, wrath, strife, seditions, heresies, envyings, murders, drunkenness, revellings, and such like: of the which I tell you before, as I have also told you in time past, that they which do such things shall not inherit the kingdom of God" (Galatians 5:19–21).

The beauty of it all is that God does not desire that anyone should perish (2 Peter 3:9), hence He provided the way out—believe in Jesus Christ and confess your sin to God, repenting of it. The scripture says that if we confess our sins, God is faithful and just to forgive us our sins and to cleanse us from all unrighteousness (1 John 1:9). When you repent[3] and put your faith in Christ, you shall be saved and your sin forgiven. Repentance includes righting a wrong where possible. Realize that you have been living in sin, and repent of it to right the wrong in your life by formalizing or legitimizing your relationship to make your partner-in-sin your husband or wife, as the case may be.

In some cultures, especially in Africa, when a man dies without properly marrying the mother of his children, the woman reverts the children to her parents, and they begin to bear the woman's maiden name unless the late man's family rises up to pay the woman's bride

---

[2] Jerry Bridges, *The Pursuit of Holiness* (Colorado Springs: NavPress, 2006), 65.

[3] *Practical Word Studies in the New Testament* defines *repentance* as "turning away from sin and turning toward God; to turn one's life around." It further explains repentance, among other explanations, as "resolving never to think or do a thing again" (p. 1723).

price and perform other relevant marriage rites. Serious as this may appear, it cannot be compared to spending eternity in hell. If the Word of God says that fornicators will go to hell, be afraid because it is true! So get saved from eternal damnation. Do not take God's love and mercy for granted.

9.3 Unmarried Single Parents

As society now promotes and supports sexual promiscuity by legalizing abortion and allowing children access to condoms, which do fail at times, many teenagers and young women become pregnant unprepared; teenage boys and very young men become fathers unprepared too. In many cases a baby is born and left with its grandmother to nurse. When Grandma is not available, the young mother or father begins to singlehandedly parent the baby.

Sexual intercourse is for the married. It is legitimate only in marriage and between legally married persons. Sex outside marriage is known as fornication or sexual immorality, which is a sin before God. The Bible says, "For you may be sure of this, that everyone who is sexually immoral or impure, or who is covetous (that is, an idolater), has no inheritance in the kingdom of Christ and God" (Ephesians 5:5 ESV).

Even though you have, and care for, the baby, you remain an immoral person until you repent of the sin and confess it to God. Jesus Christ said that He will in no wise cast out anyone who comes to Him (John 6:37b). Prayerfully plan and get married when you are mature in mind, so as to stop running a single-parent family and to properly bring up your child and any other children that God may give you in the fear and admonition of the Lord.

9.4 Separated and Divorced Couples/Parents

More often than not, separation leads to divorce. Though it is believed that separated couples may reunite, it is dangerous to allow separation to set into a marriage. It is said that only about 13 percent of separated couples get reunited, whereas about 86 percent of such couples progress (or better, retrogress) to divorce. The reason is that once apart, they can no longer pray together, and the devil magnifies and builds on the cause of separation, making the couple enjoy separation, especially by introducing foreigners into the lives of the separated persons. Gradually reconciliation becomes an uphill task, impossible and permanent, until one of the two goes to an authority (usually the court) to formally dissolve the marriage, which such authority has no divine authority to do so.

The Word quotes the Lord, the God of Israel, saying that He hates divorce! "To divorce your wife is to overwhelm her with cruelty," says the Lord of heaven's armies. So a man is required to guard his heart and not be unfaithful to his wife (Malachi 2:16 NLT). Although the verse talks about the man who divorces his wife, the opposite case (i.e., where a wife divorces her husband) is also true, especially these days. Divorce must not be named after anyone who fears or respects God, "for our God is a consuming fire" (Hebrews 12:29). Moses told the people of Israel on their way to the Promised Land, "For the Lord thy God is a consuming fire, even a jealous God" (Deuteronomy 4:24). Other passages where the almighty God was so described include the following:

> *Thou shalt not make thee any graven image, or any likeness of any thing that is in heaven above, or that is in the earth beneath, or that is in the waters beneath the earth: Thou shalt not bow down thyself unto them, nor serve them: for I the Lord thy God am a jealous God, visiting the iniquity of the fathers upon the children unto the third and fourth generation of them that hate me, And shewing mercy unto thousands of them that love me and keep my commandments. (Deuteronomy 5:8–10)*

132

And ye shall perish among the heathen, and the land of your enemies shall eat you up. And they that are left of you shall pine away in their iniquity in your enemies' lands; and also in the iniquities of their fathers shall they pine away with them. If they shall confess their iniquity, and the iniquity of their fathers, with their trespass which they trespassed against me, and that also they have walked contrary unto me. (Leviticus 26:38–40)

And it shall come to pass, when thou shalt shew this people all these words, and they shall say unto thee, Wherefore hath the Lord pronounced all this great evil against us? or what is our iniquity? or what is our sin that we have committed against the Lord our God? Then shalt thou say unto them, Because your fathers have forsaken me, saith the Lord, and have walked after other gods, and have served them, and have worshipped them, and have forsaken me, and have not kept my law; And ye have done worse than your fathers; for, behold, ye walk every one after the imagination of his evil heart, that they may not hearken unto me. (Jeremiah 16:10–12)

Depending on the age at which a couple acquire a divorce, every divorced person is very likely to engage in adulterous practices for the rest of his or her life, as it is tough for human nature to stay free of the company of someone of the opposite sex. Let's be reminded of the teachings of the Lord Jesus Christ on adultery, as follows:

- "But I say unto you, That whosoever shall put away his wife, saving for the cause of fornication, causeth her to commit adultery: and whosoever shall marry her that is divorced committeth adultery" (Matthew 5:32; Mark 10:11).
- "And I say unto you, Whosoever shall put away his wife, except it be for fornication, and shall marry another,

committeth adultery: and whoso marrieth her which is put away doth commit adultery" (Matthew 19:9).

• "And if a woman shall put away her husband, and be married to another, she committeth adultery" (Mark 10:12).

The Word of God says in 1 Thessalonians 5:22 to flee all appearance of evil, bearing in mind that fornicators and adulterers shall not inherit the kingdom of God.

> *Now the works of the flesh are manifest, which are these; adultery, fornication, uncleanness, lasciviousness, idolatry, witchcraft, hatred, variance, emulations, wrath, strife, seditions, heresies, envyings, murders, drunkenness, revellings, and such like: of the which I tell you before, as I have also told you in time past, that they which do such things shall not inherit the kingdom of God. (Galatians 5:19–21)*

Also, separation and divorce lead to loneliness generally, which sometimes ends in depression and death, including death by suicide. Children may keep a divorced parent company in the meantime. Not all adult experiences may be shared with one's children, and sooner or later the children take leave of the parent to pursue higher education or to start their own homes. At this point in the life of the divorced parent, loneliness begins to set in, in a more pronounced manner than ever. Why do you allow loneliness to kill you if your ex- spouse is still living and not remarried? Get reconciled and avoid the past mistakes that led to your current circumstance. Cast your mind back to those good old days and times when you loved each other to the extent of deciding to be for each other, and relive those times.

No sin against any person is unforgivable! In the model prayer that Jesus Christ taught His disciples, you find in verse 12 of Matthew 6, "*And forgive us our debts, as we forgive our debtors*" (emphasis added). You are a hypocrite each time you recite this while still being divorced from your spouse. Jesus went on to say in verses 14 and 15 that the reason is that if you forgive people their trespasses, your heavenly Father will also forgive you; but if you fail to forgive people their trespasses, your Father will not forgive your trespasses either.

Ask yourself whether you have become sinless such that you no longer need God's forgiveness. What did your spouse do to you that cannot be forgiven, for which reason you are ready to forgo God's forgiveness and all its attendant benefits? Forgoing God's forgiveness of your sins has eternal consequences. When Peter asked Jesus Christ how often (how many times) he should forgive his brother, suggesting seven times, Jesus Christ answered that He says not to him "until seven times: but, Until seventy times seven" (Matthew 18:22). That is 490 times, likely in one day. If God forgives you as you confess your sin to Him in repentance, you too should forgive your spouse. You might say that such a thing is easier said than done. But anything you possess, such as ego, wealth, or prestige, can be forgone for the sake of making it to heaven and reciprocating the love of God in Christ. Jesus Christ taught, "And if your hand or your foot causes you to sin, cut it off and throw it away. It is better for you to enter life crippled or lame than with two hands or two feet to be thrown into the eternal fire. And if your eye causes you to sin, tear it out and throw it away. It is better for you to enter life with one eye than with two eyes to be thrown into the hell of fire" (Matthew 18:8–9 ESV).

If Jesus Christ left all in heaven for your sake, why can you not do the same for the sake of your (erstwhile) loved one? Be reconciled to your spouse. Eschew all forms of bitterness. Do it in the fear, and for the sake, of God—because He hates your present status. He loves you and does not want you to perish. Heaven is too precious a place to miss for the sake of some man or woman. If it appears too hard for you, go back in prayer to the Author of marriage—GOD. "Pride goeth before destruction, and an haughty spirit before a fall" (Proverbs 16:18). Do not be too proud to give God a chance in your life and the respect due Him. He is the Author of life and marriage.

Suppose a man acquired an estate, designed the structure of the houses he wanted to be built on the estate, and gave people authority to build their own houses on the estate. If anyone went on to build houses with structures that differed from the standard structure given, the estate owner would surely disapprove of those houses. He might choose to punish or discipline the offender, up to the point of demolishing the houses.

Although God is not human and does not think or behave like mankind, notwithstanding that He created mankind in His image, yet He said, "For I the Lord thy God am a jealous God, visiting the iniquity of the fathers upon the children unto the third and fourth generation of them that hate me; and shewing mercy unto thousands of them that love me, and keep my commandments" (Exodus 20:5–6).

As the Lord ordained marriage, the structure He chose for it and authorized was one man, one wife. Genesis 1:27 notes: "So God created man in his own image, in the image of God created he him; male and female created he them." Also consider Jesus Christ's teaching: "Have ye not read, that he which made them at the beginning made them male and female, And said, For this cause shall a man leave father and mother, and shall cleave to his wife: and they twain shall be one flesh? Wherefore they are no more twain, but one flesh. What therefore God hath joined together, let not man put asunder" (Matthew 19:4–6).

From Genesis to Revelation, there has not yet been found any verse that indicates that God has changed the structure of marriage. Let us therefore endeavor to maintain God's structure for marriage as a way to please Him in and with our lives. It remains one man, one wife!

Do not live in sin or make someone else do so. Repent of and confess any sin in your life, and make restitution where necessary.

The songwriter wrote/prayed, "God, give us Christian homes!"[4]

God give us Christian homes!
Homes where the Bible is loved and taught,
Homes where the Master's will is sought,
Homes crowned with beauty Your love has wrought;
God give us Christian homes;
God give us Christian homes!

God give us Christian homes!
Homes where the father is true and strong,
Homes that are free from the blight of wrong,
Homes that are joyous with love and song; God
give us Christian homes;
God give us Christian homes!

God give us Christian homes!
Homes where the mother, in caring quest,
Strives to show others Your way is best,
Homes where the Lord is an honored guest;
God give us Christian homes;
God give us Christian homes!

God give us Christian homes!
Homes where the children are led to know
Christ in His beauty who loves them so,
Homes where the altar fires burn and glow;
God give us Christian homes;
God give us Christian homes!

---

[4] Baylus B. McKinney, *Baptist Hymnal* (Nashville: Convention Press, 1975), 397.

SOURCES

Books

Barclay, William. *The Letters to Timothy, Titus, and Philemon.* Philadelphia: Westminster Press, 1975.

Bridges, Jerry. *The Pursuit of Holiness.* Colorado Springs: NavPress, 2006.

Cobble, Dorothy Sue, Linda Gordon, and Astrid Henry. *Feminism Unfinished: A Short, Surprising History of American Women's Movements.* New York: Liveright, 2014.

Gipp, Samuel C. *Gipp's Understandable History of the Bible.* Miamitown, OH: DayStar, 2004.

Gundry, Robert H. *A Survey of the New Testament.* Grand Rapids, MI: Zondervan, 1994.

Inrig, Gary. *God's Mysterious Ways.* Grand Rapids, MI: Discovery House, 2016.

Ironside, H. A. *James and Peter.* Neptune, NJ: Loizeaux Brothers, 1972.

Koh, Leslie. "Friday, November 23, 2018." In *Our Daily Bread.* Grand Rapids, MI: Our Daily Bread Ministries, 2018.

LaPierre, Scott. *Marriage God's Way.* Woodland, WA: Charis Family Publishing, 2016.

McDaniel, R. H., and Charles H. Gabriel. "Since Jesus Came into My Heart." In *The New National Baptist Hymnal.* Nashville: National Baptist Publishing Board, 1977.

McKinney, Baylus B. *Baptist Hymnal.* Nashville: Convention Press, 1975.

Moo, Douglas J. *The Letters to the Colossians and to Philemon.* Grand Rapids, MI: William B. Eerdmans, 2008.

The Pastor's Handbook, rev. ed. Chicago: Wing Spread, 2006.

Practical Word Studies in the New Testament, Volume 2: L–Z. Chattanooga: Leadership Ministries Worldwide, 1998.

Syms, Walter Hynes. "God, Give Us Christian Homes!" In *Baptist Hymnal*, edited by B. B. McKinney. Nashville: Convention Press, 1956.

Thomsen, Natasha. *Global Issues: Women's Rights.* New York: Facts on File, 2007.

Walvoord, John F., and Roy B. Zuck, eds. *The Bible Knowledge Commentary: Epistles and Prophecy.* Colorado Springs: David C. Cook, 1983, 2018.

Webster's All-in-One Dictionary and Thesaurus. 2008 Edition

Woods, Guy N. *A Commentary on the New Testament Epistles of Peter, John, and Jude.* Nashville: Gospel Advocate Company, 1973.

Websites

"Feminist Movement." Wikipedia. Last updated April 24, 2018. https://en.wikipedia.org/wiki/Feminist_Movement.

Freeman, Jo. "The Women's Liberation Movement: Its Origins, Structures, and Ideas." Accessed April 30, 2018. http://www.jofreeman.com/feminism/liberationmov.htm.

Accessed April 24, 2018. https://www.thoughtco.com/womens-liberation-movement-3528926.

Accessed July 8, 2018. http://biblehub.com/commentaries/cambridge/ephesians/5.htm.

Accessed July 8, 2018. http://biblehub.com/commentaries/barnes/ephesians/5.htm.

Accessed July 6, 2018. https://biblehub.com/commentaries/pulpit/1
    peter/3.htm.
Accessed July 5, 2018. https://biblehub.com/commentaries/vws/1
    peter/3.htm.
Accessed July 5, 2018. https://biblehub.com/commentaries/poole/1
    peter/3.htm.

Articles

Jennifer Wolf. "The Single Parent Statistics Based on Census Data,"
    Accessed November 11, 2019. https://www.verywellfamily.com/
    single-parent-census-data-2997668
The Space-out Scientist. "Single parents worldwide: Statistics and
    trends," Accessed November 11, 2019. https://spacedout
    scientist.com/2017/07/18/single-parents-worldwide-statistics-
    and-trends/.
Winfree, Paul. "How Welfare Spending Hurts the People It's
    Supposed to Help." *The Daily Signal,* August 1, 2015.
    https://www.dailysignal.com/2015/08/01/how-welfare-
    spending-hurts-the-people-its-supposed-to-help/.

APPENDIX

Some Poems by the Author

What Shall I Render?

Refrain:[1] I will praise You, Lord, And
shout Hallelujah.
What shall I render to You, my God?

    1.   What shall I render?
What shall I render?
What shall I render to You, oh Lord? (Refrain.)

    2.   I'll render praises. I'll
render worship;
I'll render honor to You, oh Lord.
(Refrain.)

    3.   I'll give my money; I'll
give materials;
I'll give my service to You, oh Lord.
(Refrain.)

---

[1] The author of the refrain and of stanza 1 is unknown.

4. I'll give thanksgiving And
adoration
And all the glory to You, oh Lord.
(Refrain.)

Stanzas 2 to 4 by Dan Nwaelene
Aseese, June 27, 2009, 12:40 a.m.

The Real Powerful Man

A real powerful man is not the man that kills! A
real powerful man means what he says, Says what
he means,
Tames and bridles his tongue.
He not only makes annual resolutions But
also keeps them to year end.
He rejects his desire
For things unhealthy to his body.

A real powerful man wins by loving. He
avoids what God's Word says is sin
And does what the Word says God loves. Jesus
Christ is the real powerful Man.
Three times the tempter tried Him in the desert. Three
times He rejected his offers,
Quoting God's Word: "It is written."
The fourth time, at Gethsemane, He
opted for God's will to be done.

Are you a powerful man?
Mean today to close your appetite
To habits that pollute the Holy Spirit's temple, Which
could destroy your body.
Request the Spirit of God today To
replace them with, by, Himself. Then
you shall be a powerful man
Because you control your appetite— Your
desires and utterances.
Ask and you shall receive.

Yonkers, New York, November 26, 2012, 9:00 a.m.

145

Thanks Be to God!

When things always work as planned,
There is joy in the total man and in the home; There's
mutual respect for all.
Love is agape, real and reciprocal; Fear
and distrust are absent; Friends always
remember you;
"Brother" is real and strong at church; Man's
help is readily available.

When life turns its other side toward you,   For
no matter for how long or short,
Joy gives way to mechanical happiness; Respect
becomes a hard buy and is demanded; Agape love
gives way to just love;
Friends no longer remember yesterday;
Even brethren adjust their distance; Hisses
become commonplace at home; Man's
help is far-fetched.

That's when you realize
That only GOD sticks around In all
circumstances.
He reminds you to trust Him alone For
there's still hope;
He'll neither leave you nor forsake you. Hence
you'll rise again.
I shall rise and shine again! *Amen.*
Thanks be to God,
The fall was not below the ground!

Aseese, Nigeria, October 4, 2009, 12:25 a.m.

Tomorrow May Be Too Late!

I am a sinner, sinner by nature,
Because all have sinned
And fall short of the glory of GOD. Hence I
was doomed eternally.

I've become a saint, saint by Christ Jesus. For
He gave His life as a ransom
That whoever believes in Him
Should have life eternal.

You too can become a saint now
By inviting Jesus Christ into your life, Your
Savior and Lord to be,
For today is the day of salvation.

He is waiting, willing, and ready To
save you now
And give you life eternal.
Tomorrow may be too late.

                                Aseese, Nigeria, April 14, 2009

Lord, Speak Your Word to Me.
(Tune: "God, Give Us Christian Homes")[2]

1.   Lord, speak Your Word to me In
such a way that it's clear to me,
In such a way that I understand, In
such a way that I may believe. Lord,
speak Your Word to me.
Lord, speak Your Word to me.

2.   Lord, let me know Your Word In
such a way that I'll do Your Word, In
such a way it can change my life, In such
a way I can speak Your Word. Lord, speak
Your Word to me.
Make Your Word known to me.

3.   Lord, may I speak Your Word In
such a way that it can be heard,
In such a way that it will be clear,
So that the hearers may know and do. Lord,
speak Your Word to me.
Make Your Word known to me.

Note: This is a good prayer to say before reading and/or preaching the
Word of God.

Westchester Medical Center, Valhalla, New
York, April 22, 2017, 8:40 a.m.

---

[2] Walter Hynes Sims, "God, Give Us Christian Homes!" In *Baptist Hymnal*, ed. B.
B. McKinney (Nashville: Convention Press, 1956), 377.

Jesus Christ

The blood of Jesus Christ
Cleanses us from all unrighteousness.
By it, Jesus saves us from hell if we believe in Him. "By
His stripes we are healed."
God gave Him a name above every name, That
at the mention of His name
Every knee must bow everywhere. He
is seated in heaven above, And so
He's above all
And all things are subject to Him.

Believe in His shed blood
And be saved from eternal death.
Cleanse your heart of every sin And all
unrighteousness.
Apply His stripes today to your sick body.
Subject all your fears and worries
To His mighty name.
Give thanks, praise, and glory To
God the Father in the name Jesus
Christ, Immanuel. Amen.

Westchester Medical Center, Valhalla, New
York, October 10, 2014, 9:30 a.m.

I Know the GOD I Serve

I know the GOD I serve.
He lives from eternity to eternity. He is
ever present.
He is ever faithful. He
lives forevermore.

I know the GOD I serve. He
is the almighty GOD He is the
omniscient One.
He created all things anywhere, everywhere.   He
lives forevermore.

I know the GOD I serve.
He knows my joys and pains. He
is in my every situation. He
rekindles my hope daily. He lives
forevermore.

I know the GOD I serve. He
loves me so much,
He gave His only Son to die for me. He'll
never, never leave or forsake me. He lives
forevermore.

I know the GOD I serve:
The Father of my Lord Jesus Christ. Though
I often fail Him,
And all men may forsake me, He'll
love me till the end.

Aseese, Nigeria, April 4, 2009, 10:00 p.m.

I Cannot But Smile (Smiley!)
(Could be sung to the tune of "What a Wonderful Change in My Life
Has Been Wrought"[3])

1. When I have Jesus Christ And
He's Lord of my life,
I cannot but smile all the time. If
I'm up or I'm down
And remember His words,
I cannot but smile all the time.

    * Chorus:
    I cannot but smile all the time; I
    cannot but smile all the time. I
    have peace in my heart,
    I have joy in my heart,
    Since Jesus is Lord of my life.

2. Jesus said to His own, "I'll
never forsake you."
I cannot but smile all the time. He
has promised to give
To me life abundant.
I cannot but smile all the time.
        (Chorus.)

3. When I think of His deeds For
to save me from hell,
I cannot but smile all the time.
When I know I'll fore'er

---

[3] R. H. McDaniel and Charles H. Gabriel, "Since Jesus Came into My Heart,"
In *The New National Baptist Hymnal* (Nashville: National Baptist Publishing
Board, 1977), 301.

Reign, yes reign, with my Lord, I
cannot but smile all the time.
        (Chorus.)

    4. Just believe in your heart He's
your Savior and Lord.
You cannot but smile all the way. And
you'll never perish;
You'll have life eternal.
You cannot but smile all the way.
        (Chorus.)

Westchester Medical Center, Valhalla, New York, October 7, 2014

Small and Great Sins

All "small" sins are small enough To
separate us from God
As much, or in the same way, as
All "great" sins are great enough to do.
All sins are, therefore, equal before God and
Have death as their wages,
But are forgivable only by confession,
Repentance, and faith in Jesus Christ,

Leading to eternal life—a gift of God.

Yonkers, New York, November 19, 2012

God Is Ever Faithful!

There's only one Relative who helps To
bear one's burden
Without complaining or grumbling. His
name is Jesus Christ.
He never quits in troubled times.

Siblings may get tired and withdraw; Parents
may get too unhappy
And ask you to leave; Children
may get too tired Or too
frustrated and quit.

Friends may consider
They personally gain nothing directly And
abandon you.
Neighbors may never have cared. But
Jesus never leaves.

He says, "I Am with you always. I'll
never leave you or forsake you."
Whatever my situation may be,
I'll keep trusting my Friend, Jesus. O
Lord, help me in my weakness.

Yonkers, New York, January 30, 2012

Pain, Go Away

Oh, this pain, please go away. Pain,
pain, go away.
Go away in Jesus' name.

Little pain, you go away. Pain,
pain, go away.
Never come another day.

Serious pain, you go away. Pain,
pain, go away.
Go away in Jesus' name.

God's Word says that I am healed.
Pain, pain, go away,
Go away in Jesus' name.

Yonkers, New York, June 2, 2019, 1:00 a.m.

155

Family Structure by Choice: A Defense of Traditional Marriage Structure by Rev. Dr. Daniel Ukadike Nwaelene, ThD, is a landmark work that arrives at a moment of global crisis for the family. It is both a prophetic warning and a pastoral guidebook, combining theological depth, cultural analysis, and practical application. In a society where divorce is normalized, single parenting by choice is increasingly common, and alternative family structures are celebrated without reflection, this book stands with clarity, conviction, and compassion, calling readers back to God's original design.

From the outset, the author establishes that the family is not the product of human culture or social evolution, but the deliberate creation of God. Any attempt to redefine, redesign, or dismantle it leads to disorder and destruction. This conviction frames the entire work and provides the foundation for its detailed exploration of marriage, parenting, and family structures across both biblical and contemporary contexts. Unlike many modern treatments of this subject, Family Structure by Choice does not rely on scattered proof texts. Instead, it consistently presents full passages of Scripture, ensuring that the weight of authority rests on the Word of God itself rather than on personal opinion.

The opening chapters set the tone with a blend of cultural realism and biblical truth. The author recalls the disturbing ease with which divorce is advertised today, contrasting it with the covenantal permanence commanded by Christ in Matthew 19:6. He reflects on his own childhood in Nigeria, where honesty and moral discipline were once upheld, and contrasts that with the rise of corruption, violence, and immorality in modern times. These observations remind readers that the decline of the family is not just a Western issue but a global one, underscoring the universality of the problem and the necessity of a biblical solution.

Chapter 2, "The Devil Is Against God and God's Work," is especially striking in its boldness. While sociologists often frame family breakdown in terms of economics or politics, the author names the true adversary: Satan himself, who wages war against the family as part of his larger battle against God's creation. The book demonstrates how divorce, immorality, and rejection of marriage are not neutral trends but spiritual strategies designed to destabilize both individuals and societies. Yet the chapter ends with hope, rooting its message in Genesis 3:15, the promise that the seed of the woman will crush the serpent's head. This section makes clear that, although the battle is real, the victory belongs to Christ.

The book's centerpiece, Chapter 3, "Marriage Was God's Idea," is one of its strongest contributions. It grounds marriage firmly in Genesis, reminding readers that marriage is not a cultural invention but a divine institution established at creation. This chapter carefully addresses exceptions such as divorce, widowhood, and single mothers, showing both the brokenness of human experience and the enduring perfection of God's design. The warnings against immorality, drawn from Proverbs, are powerful and relevant, speaking with as much urgency to today's readers as they did to ancient Israel. The message is clear: marriage is sacred, instituted by God, and essential for human flourishing.

Chapters 4 and 5 expand the discussion by addressing modern realities. Chapter 4, "Family Structures Today, Mankind's Creation," catalogs polygamy, polyandry, same-sex marriage, cohabitation, and blurred parental roles, showing how each represents a departure from God's plan. These sections are written with clarity and conviction but also with compassion, acknowledging the human stories behind these choices while remaining faithful to biblical truth. Chapter 5, "Reasons for Avoidance of Marriage," highlights the fears that prevent many young adults from marrying: fear of abuse, infertility, finances, loss of freedom, and the influence of feminist ideology. These fears are treated with empathy, but the author demonstrates how rejecting marriage out of fear aligns with the deception warned of in 1 Timothy 4. The balance of understanding and truth in these chapters is a defining strength of the book.

The pastoral heart of the work shines through in Chapters 6 through 9. Chapter 6, "The Making of Single Parents," distinguishes between unavoidable circumstances, such as death, sickness, imprisonment, or war, and chosen circumstances, such as immorality, divorce, impatience, misogyny, and misandry. Compassion is shown to those caught in tragedy, while firm admonition is given to those who reject God's design by choice. Chapter 7, "The Ideal Family in God's View," is one of the most comprehensive biblical portraits of family available. Drawing from the teachings of Jesus, Paul, and Peter, the author paints a picture of the family as a covenant of love, submission, honor, and mutual responsibility. The reminder that husbands and wives are heirs together of the grace of life, and that even their prayers can be hindered by disunity, is both convicting and inspiring.

Chapter 8, "Effects of Single Parenting by Choice," addresses the consequences of chosen family breakdown with sobering honesty. The effects on children, parents, society, and the church are carefully detailed, leaving no doubt that rejecting God's design leads to pain and instability at every level. Chapter 9, "Conclusions and Recommendations," ensures the book does not end in despair but in hope and direction. Here, practical guidance is offered for young people, unmarried or cohabiting parents, single parents, and divorced couples. These recommendations are not simplistic solutions but thoughtful, pastoral instructions rooted in both Scripture and lived experience.

The overall strength of Family Structure by Choice lies in its ability to combine biblical authority with cultural relevance, theological depth with pastoral care, and bold conviction with genuine compassion. It is not merely a book of diagnosis but also one of prescription, pointing readers toward repentance, reconciliation, and restoration through God's grace. Its message is timeless, yet urgently timely for a generation in danger of losing its moral and spiritual compass.

This book deserves to be regarded as essential reading. Every Christian household should have a copy. Every pastor and church leader should keep it as a resource for counseling and teaching. Young adults preparing for marriage should study it carefully, and even those outside the church will find in it a compelling argument for why the family remains the nucleus of society. To ignore its message is to risk drifting through life's most important decisions without guidance. To embrace it is to secure a foundation that aligns with God's eternal wisdom.

Verdict: Family Structure by Choice is powerful, prophetic, and profoundly necessary. A work that should be in every home, every church, and every community seeking to rebuild society on the firm foundation of God's design.

BOOK REVIEW BY
DONRAE MISTRY
October 2025

ABOUT THE AUTHOR

WHEN THE APOSTLE JOHN DESCRIBED HIMSELF AS THE disciple whom Jesus loved (John 13:23; 20:2; 21:7, 20, 24), he made it sound like Jesus Christ loved *nobody* else in the world but him. But in Christ there is no partiality or favoritism, as the apostle Peter said: "Of a truth I perceive that God is no respecter of persons" (Acts 10:34). The apostle Paul reiterated, "For there is no respect of persons with God" (Romans 2:11). The same John quoted Jesus Christ saying to Nicodemus, "For God so loved the world, that he gave his only begotten Son, that whosoever believeth in him should not perish, but have everlasting life" (John 3:16).

I believe, like the apostle John, that I am one of the sons of God whom Jesus Christ loves and died for. This is in view of my realization of the love, mercy, and grace of God for me in Christ Jesus. I have not been the best person, or the wisest or smartest person anywhere, yet the Lord has blessed me with some peculiar gifts for service to Him. Although I am not yet where I expected to be, I am not where I was yesterday, all by God's special grace.

I was the founding pastor of Royal Priesthood Baptist Church, Aseese, Ogun State, Nigeria, before relocating to the USA, where I did further studies and obtained a master of theology and doctor of theology degree. I am in the Lord's service as a minister (associate pastor) on a bivocational basis at Community Baptist Church, Yonkers, New York, for the fifth year, where I was ordained Before my call to the pastoral ministry, God took me though industry, where He gave me special favors, the testimonies of which are documented but not yet published. The Lord has been good to me. Meanwhile, the Holy Spirit has used me and helped me to publish two books before this one. To God be all the glory.

I am married to Patricia, and we have been blessed with two sons and two daughters. I would counsel, appeal to, and encourage you to appreciate God's love for you today, and if you have not already put your trust in His only begotten Son Jesus Christ, invite Him into your heart and life and be saved, "For he saith, I have heard thee in a time accepted, and in the day of salvation have I succoured thee: behold, now is the accepted time; behold, now is the day of salvation" (2 corinthians 6:2).